Heaven, By Hotel Standards

THE HISTORY OF THE OMNI PARKER HOUSE

BY SUSAN WILSON

FOR HARVEY

ISBN 978-0-615-93497-6
Library of Congress Control Number 2013957514
Printed in the USA

Design: Nieshoff Design / Lexington, MA • www.nieshoffdesign.com

CONTENTS

Introduction by Susan Wilson, House Historian 4

Preface by Thomas P. O'Neill III 6

Welcome Message from John Murtha, General Manager 8

The History of the Omni Parker House 10

Welcome to the Neighborhood 13

Wild About Harvey 17

Food for Thought 26

Guess Who's Coming to Dinner? 42

      Literary Liaisons 44

      Party Politics 54

      Theatrical Pursuits 64

Architecturally Speaking 78

Building a Better Parker House 84

Spectral Evidence 98

Parker Coat of Arms 102

About the Author & Designer 104

Time After Time: Omni Parker House
Historic Timeline, Maps, and Celebrated Guests

Photo Credits 105

Index 107

INTRODUCTION

In March of 1877, humorist Mark Twain was staying at the Parker House in room 168. A reporter from the Globe entered Twain's room, shuttled in by a porter. After a pause of several moments, Twain swiveled around in his large easy chair and faced his visitor. With a local newspaper in hand and puffing on a large cigar, Twain observed to the reporter, "You see for yourself that I'm pretty near heaven—not theologically, of course, but by the hotel standard."

Times have changed since Samuel Clemens' popular "Mark Twain" persona entertained the media. In many ways, however, the Omni Parker House has not.

Though the Parker House has been a Boston destination since 1855 (and an "Omni" since 1984), it has continually managed to straddle the past and the present with aplomb. One could easily repeat today the words written by a *Boston Globe* reporter in 1927: "Despite the fact that the new hotel is modern in every way, the traditions, spirit, and general atmosphere of the old Parker House, beloved by countless Bostonians and visitors from other cities, have been retained."

As a child growing up in New Jersey, I experienced the legendary Parker House Roll, thanks to the baking talents of my mother. As an undergraduate and graduate student at Tufts University, I partook of Parker House glories first hand—not only the rolls, but also the "Bloody Mary Fountains" that commenced at the stroke of noon for Sunday brunch.

Then I got serious.

In the early 1990s, I began researching and writing about the Omni Parker House, starting with my "Sites and Insights" column in the *Boston Globe* (followed by my book of the same name). Over the years, I had the opportunity to write and photograph various pieces about or for the hotel, as well as do TV shows, tours, and lectures on its fascinating past and present. Then, in the summer of 2012, General Manager John Murtha made me an offer I couldn't refuse: the task of creating the ultimate compendium of all those years of study—a hefty new volume of images and stories, which, inspired by Mr. Twain, we elected to call *Heaven, By Hotel Standards*.

This book is the happy result.

There are numerous individuals and institutions I want to thank for their knowledge, time, assistance, and expertise. First and foremost, I want to credit John Murtha for having the vision and for finding the resources to make this book happen. Thanks also to Dave Ritchie, Ruth Dwyer, and Lori Tower of the Omni Parker House for their help and faith in me and the project—and for always being there. We were so fortunate that Tom O'Neill agreed to recount his family history for the book preface.

In the greater Boston area, I am forever indebted to Bo, Bill, and Annette Winiker of Winiker Music, Jill Person of Person + Killian Photography, Meg Winslow of Mount Auburn Cemetery, and Aaron Schmidt of the Boston Public Library. Special thanks to Will and Joan Dunfey, Eleanor Dunfey-Freiburger, Jerry Dunfey, Arthur Pollack of the *Boston Herald*, Maryrose Grossman of the John Fitzgerald Kennedy Presidential Library and Museum, Kristen Swett and Marta Crilly of the City of Boston Archives, Phil Bergen of the Massachusetts Historical Commission, Stephanie Loeb Stepanek and Julie Frey of the Museum of Fine Arts, Boston, Lisa Long Feldmann of the Isabella Stewart Gardner Museum, Elaine Doran of the Lexington Historical Society, the staff of the Schlesinger Library on the History of Women in America, and Eddie Cotto and Seamus Murphy of the Omni Parker House staff.

My great friends and Boston history colleagues Nancy S. Seasholes, James Vrabel, Polly Flansburgh (who connected me with architect John Clemson), Charlie Bahne, and Martha S. Hassell, Dean of the New England School of Photography, provided essential clues, facts, links, comments, edits, images, or encouragement throughout the project. And my neighbor, Lea Dugan, pushed me to pursue the truth behind the Stephen King legend.

In pursuing obscure and unheralded facts about founder Harvey Parker and longtime Parker House proprietor J. Reed Whipple in particular, I made a lot of friends and contacts "Up No'th." Unlimited praises to the creative crew from New Boston, New Hampshire—Dick Moody, Lisa Rothman, Dan Rothman, and Nonah Poole of the New Boston Historical Society. My Maine contingent included excellent factual finds from Jamie Kingman Rice of the Maine Historical Society, Betsy Graves of Temple, Maine, and Ben B. Conant of Paris, Maine.

Both Kirsten Carter of the Franklin D. Roosevelt Presidential Library & Museum in Hyde Park, New York, and Mervet Sweiss of the White Coffee Company of Astoria, New York, helped me wade through some important myths and mysteries.

Finally, I was especially pleased to be able to access the rich online photographic archives of two of America's national treasures: The National Archives and the Library of Congress.

It's always a pleasure to collaborate with Pat Nieshoff of Nieshoff Design in Lexington, with whom I have co-created various books and brochures since 1997. Lastly, kudos to Rebecca Strauss and Emma Thompson Strauss-Wilson, who are always there, always supportive, and always willing to put up with my obsessions—most notably, this beloved Omni Parker House.

Susan Wilson
House Historian

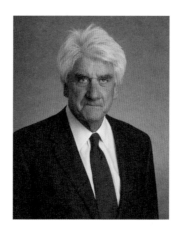

PREFACE

by Thomas P. O'Neill III

Located steps from Old City Hall and King's Chapel Cemetery, the Parker House tells its own story about Boston's history and the cultural, economic and political changes that have taken place since it opened its doors on School Street in 1855.

My memories of the Parker House begin almost 100 years after its initial opening, in the 1940s when I would occasionally join my father and then-Governor of Massachusetts, Paul Dever, for lunch. At the time, my father was Speaker of the House for the State of Massachusetts, and lunch at the Parker House with Governor Dever was a weekly tradition. There were only five restaurants in the city of Boston back then, a number that would not change significantly until the renaissance of the 1960s and 1970s under Mayor Kevin White.

After the Parker House was purchased by the Dunfey family in 1968, I built even more memories there as an active member of the New England Circle, a talking and listening group that met at the Parker House to discuss social and political issues. One memory that stands out is when the Circle hosted Gerry Adams, President of Sinn Féin in Ireland, on his second ever visit to the U.S. While I recall having 40-50 participants at earlier meetings of the Circle, this event drew a crowd of two-to-three-hundred.

I remained involved in the Circle from the 1970s until the 1990s, becoming a sponsor at the end of the 1980s after I had left politics. Along with the memories and friendships I built there as a member of the Circle, the Parker House was the

Tom O'Neill confers with his father, "Tip" O'Neill.

site of other important milestones over the years. It was there that I announced my candidacy for Lieutenant Governor of Massachusetts in 1974. It was also at the Parker House that my father held his last fundraiser, which was for the Democratic Congressional Campaign Committee in 1987 and raised over $100,000.

These decades of memories represent only a sliver of the history that the Parker House has seen. The hotel was there for events that shaped Boston and its future, including the Civil War, the Great Fire of 1872 and the Boston Police Strike of 1919. The Parker House saw the days of old Scollay Square, and it has been host to historical figures such as Ho Chi Minh and Malcolm X.

When I was Lieutenant Governor, the Parker House was one of the few hotels in the Greater Boston area, housing 3,500 rooms. Today, by contrast, there are about 58,000 hotel rooms in Greater Boston. This estimate alone demonstrates the tremendous changes that have taken place around the Parker House in recent decades, not to mention since its opening over 150 years ago.

As Boston continues to evolve, the Parker House—renamed the Omni Parker House in 1984—remains an important part of the city's fabric. It is only by understanding the hotel's rich and lengthy history that one can truly grasp its importance to Boston and to our entire state. Located in one of Boston's most historic neighborhoods, the Parker House remains an iconic landmark not to be forgotten.

WELCOME FROM
THE OMNI PARKER HOUSE

by John Murtha CHA, General Manager

WE BELIEVE THAT THIS NEW AND GREATLY ENHANCED VERSION OF OUR HISTORY BOOK is a fitting way to celebrate the 30th anniversary of the Parker House as a member of the Omni Hotels & Resorts collection of hotels. Although visiting our property is the best way to experience our history, we hope the book will inspire you to stay with us in the future, meet our associates, and explore the city of Boston right outside our door.

This book would not have been possible without its author, our own "house historian," Susan Wilson. Her professional approach in uncovering so many interesting aspects of our history, along with her passion for authenticity and detail, make her a very special partner in preserving the legacy of our unique hotel.

We hope you will enjoy *Heaven, By Hotel Standards*.

Modern Day Parker House General Managers

John Murtha	2007 - present	Robert McIntosh	1976 - 1980
Richard Mason	2000 - 2007	Yervant Chekijian	1974 - 1976
John Hopkins	1999 - 2000	Hal Richman	1973 - 1974
Michael Knapp	1996 - 1999	James McCrindle	1972 - 1973
Paul Sacco	1993 - 1996	Frank Shelton	1971 - 1972
Laurence Jeffery	1988 - 1993	Adam Aloise	1968 - 1971
Rainer Joutz	1987 - 1988	Andrew Sherrard	1958 - 1968
Antonio Torres	1985 - 1987	Glenwood Sherrard	1933 - 1958
Philip Georgas	1980 - 1985	Claude Hart	1927 - 1932

HEAVEN, BY HOTEL STANDARDS
THE HISTORY OF THE OMNI PARKER HOUSE

Mention the name "Omni Parker House," and a century and a half of rich and varied history comes to mind. Founded by Harvey D. Parker in 1855, the Omni Parker House—located at the junction of Tremont and School streets—is the oldest of Boston's elegant inns and the longest continuously operating hotel in the United States. It was here where the brightest lights of America's Golden Age of Literature—writers like Emerson, Thoreau, Hawthorne, and Longfellow—regularly met for conversation and conviviality in the legendary nineteenth-century Saturday Club. It was here where baseball greats like Babe Ruth, Ted Williams, Carl Yastrzemski, and David Ortiz wined, dined, and unwound. And it was here, too, where generations of local and national politicians—including Ulysses S. Grant, James Michael Curley, Franklin Delano Roosevelt, John F. Kennedy, Colin Powell, William Jefferson Clinton, and Deval Patrick—assembled for private meetings, press conferences, and power breakfasts.

With its close proximity to Boston's Theater District, the Omni Parker House also played an important role for thespians. Many of the nineteenth century's finest actors made the Parker House a home away from home, including Charlotte Cushman, Sarah Bernhardt, Edwin Booth, and the latter's handsome, matinee-idol brother, John Wilkes. During the twentieth century, that list expanded to include stars of stage, screen, and television—from Joan Crawford, Judy Garland, James Dean, and William ("Hopalong Cassidy") Boyd to Adam ("Batman") West, Stevie Nicks, Kelsey Grammer, Ann-Margret, Yo-Yo Ma, Rachael Ray, and Ben Affleck.

Equally impressive are the contributions made by venerable Parker House kitchens to American culinary culture. It was talented bakers and cooks here who invented the famed Parker House Roll and perfected many of the dishes we now associate with Boston and New England cuisine. Parker's has also been the training ground for internationally-known chefs and features a top-notch kitchen and wait staff that once included Malcolm X and Ho Chi Minh.

Freedom Trail sidewalk plaque

None of this, of course, has ever been a secret. The constantly clever Oliver Wendell Homes, Sr., for example—that self-avowed "Autocrat of the Breakfast Table"—waxed eloquent on the food and friends he encountered at this most favorite of haunts:

> *Such feasts! The laughs of many a jocund hour*
> *That shook the mortar from King George's tower;*
> *Such guests! What famous names its record boasts,*
> *Whose owners wander in the mob of ghosts!*

Located along Boston's beloved Freedom Trail, today's Omni Parker House is more than a museum of American myth and memory. It's a compelling, contemporary, full-service hotel that has meticulously maintained its nineteenth-century charms and sense of history. Lobbies, bar-lounges, and restaurant alike are couched in the dark hues of yesteryear; doors and elevators gleam of freshly burnished decorative bronze, while the walls are vintage American oak. Crystal chandeliers glow above, as guests sink into oversized chairs below, in little enclaves resembling private clubrooms.

In sum, the Omni Parker House is not only a vibrant living landmark, but also a twenty-first century destination of choice. Indeed, the Parker House is still rightly called *the* Grand Dame of Boston hotels.

Tremont Street, 1843

The Bell of Boston

Alexander Graham Bell with his wife Mabel Gardiner Hubbard and their children Elsie May Bell (left) and Marian Hubbard Bell, circa 1885.

Among the prestigious patrons of the Parker House at the turn of the twentieth century was Alexander Graham Bell (1847-1922), the iconic inventor, innovator, scientist, and engineer credited with inventing the first practical telephone.

Bell, as it turns out, was no stranger to Boston.

Born and bred in Scotland, Bell first moved to The Hub in his early 20s to work at the Boston School for Deaf Mutes (now the Horace Mann School for the Deaf). Once here, he trained the school's instructors in a method of notating spoken sounds that his father had created, called the Visible Speech System. A year later the talented young Bell was made professor of Vocal Physiology and Elocution at the Boston University School of Oratory.

Dedicated to medical research and developing techniques for teaching speech to the deaf, Bell was swept up by the excitement of working amidst the numerous scientists and inventors who populated Boston. He was also swept up by one of his deaf students, Mabel Hubbard of Cambridge, a bright attractive woman ten years his junior.

Through his scientific work with vibrations, transmitters, and electromagnets, done both in Canada and the U.S., Bell was able to conceive a way to transmit human speech over a wire. One result, of course, was his invention of the telephone in 1876. The entire "Mr. Watson, come here, I want to see you" scenario happened in Boston, only a few blocks away from the Parker House.

1877 was a banner year for "Alec" Bell; he formed the Bell Telephone Company and married Mabel Hubbard. Within a decade of that watershed year, more than 150,000 people in the U.S. owned telephones. The popular nickname for Bell Telephone—"Ma" Bell—was merely a play on his wife's name.

Though Bell moved away from Boston, he often returned and often made the Parker House his hotel of choice. Among his reasons for visiting were meetings with old friends and colleagues, consulting at places like the Horace Mann School, seeing the Hubbard family, receiving honorary degrees from Harvard, and lecturing—the latter of which proved a vital source of income in the first two decades of Bell Telephone.

Since Bell was born in the United Kingdom, then resided in both Canada and the United States, all three countries claim him as their "native son." In nationwide polls, he has been voted one of the 100 Greatest Britons (2002), the 10 Greatest Canadians (2004), and the 100 Greatest Americans (2005).

School Street was named for America's first public school, which made its home here from 1645 to 1844.

WELCOME TO
THE NEIGHBORHOOD

The corner of Tremont and School streets, where the Omni Parker House has stood since 1855, is almost as old as Boston itself.

In 1630, when Englishman John Winthrop and the Puritans of the Massachusetts Bay Colony first settled here, they knew the peninsula as Trimountaine, named as such for the three hills (now remembered as Beacon, Pemberton, and Mount Vernon) that dominated the skyline. The young colony's first church, town house, freshwater spring, and stock and pillory were all located within two short blocks of where the Parker House stands today. Though the town was soon renamed Boston, to honor the Lincolnshire town that many had just departed, and though the three mountains were later leveled or substantially shortened to make new land, the early moniker lived on in the contraction, "Tremont." Tremont Street was laid out along the base of those three vintage hills and Boston Common.

The location and name of School Street also originated in Puritan times. During the years 1635-36, the British colonists established a college in nearby Cambridge (the world-renowned Harvard) and a college preparatory school in Boston. By 1645, that prep school—America's first public school—was housed in a 40-by-25-foot cabin on what came to be known as School Street. A folk-art engraving embedded in the sidewalk behind King's Chapel commemorates the institution's location from 1645 to 1748. That school, later known as Boston Latin, educated a host of Boston's brightest young males, including Sam Adams, John Hancock, Charles Bulfinch, and Ralph Waldo Emerson. Its most illustrious dropout was surely Benjamin Franklin, whose statue hovers nearby, in front of Old City Hall. The street name stayed, although Boston Latin moved on: first to the corner of School Street and Chapman Place (1748-1844), where Parker's Bar now stands, and eventually to the Fenway, where the prestigious school thrives to this day.

In colonial times, School Street was little more than a glorified dirt path to Boston Common. Boston Latin shared the street with barns, gardens, orchards, small shops, churches, livery stables, and wooden homes—and neighbors like James Otis, John Winthrop, John Winslow, Mary Chilton, Anne Hutchinson, and the alleged "witch,"

King's Chapel and the old Parker House stand at the corner of Tremont and School streets, one of Boston's oldest intersections.

In colonial Boston—long before Harvey Parker was even born—one of the best slopes for winter sledding was the ice-packed strip down Beacon and School streets. One winter, as a group of rambunctious boys tumbled out of Boston Latin School, they found that British General Frederick Haldimand's servant had spread ashes down the street, melting their precious ice. In a move that presaged the upcoming revolution, the boys protested to Haldimand, who was headquartered near the school. Haldimand apologized, chastised his servant, and instructed the latter to put water on the street every night to re-freeze the surface. When the Military Royal Governor of the Province of Massachusetts Bay, General Thomas Gage, was told of the incident, he reportedly noted, "It is impossible to beat the notion of liberty out of the people, as it has been rooted in them from childhood."

Ann Hibbins. The street's gentle slope made it a favorite sledding hill; its taverns made it a favorite drinking spot, which Lieutenant Colonel George Washington was known to frequent when visiting Boston on military and surveying jobs. As time passed, the dirt road was paved with cobblestones, and the buildings replaced with more elaborate structures. Despite such changes, two distinctive colonial-era buildings remain on School Street to this day: King's Chapel, a rough-hewn granite church completed in 1754, and the Old Corner Bookstore building—the latter constructed in 1718 as an apothecary shop and private residence.

In 1704, a mansion was built on the future site of the Omni Parker House by a wealthy Boston merchant named John Mico. After Mico's death in 1718, that elegant, three-story brick home passed on to his friend and colleague, Jacob Wendell. Wendell was the grandfather of physician and writer, Dr. Oliver Wendell Holmes, Sr., a member of the famed Saturday Club. After Jacob Wendell's death, Nicholas Boylston—a cousin of statesman John Adams—took possession of the aging Mico mansion. But by the early 1800s, the home was an eyesore: no longer a wealthy, well-maintained private residence, it instead became a boarding house, rechristened the Boylston Hotel in 1829.

It was during those years of decline that Harvey Parker came along. With him came the start of a new era: for School Street, for the city of Boston—and for the world of fine public accommodations.

In 1854, the year Harvey Parker bought the lot to build his Parker House...

- *The Governor of Massachusetts was Emery Washburn and the mayor was Jerome Van Crowninshield Smith.*

- *Franklin Pierce, an old Bowdoin College schoolmate of Nathaniel Hawthorne and Henry Wadsworth Longfellow, was President of the United States.*

- *The first Women's Rights Convention was held in Boston.*

- *The runaway slave, Anthony Burns, was captured and tried in Boston, and returned to his master in Virginia, in compliance with the Fugitive Slave Law; 50,000 Boston-area demonstrators protested his return.*

- *The Massachusetts legislature passed a law prohibiting segregation in the Boston Public Schools.*

- *The Boston Art Club was formed.*

- *Boston's population was 160,000.*

- *The Back Bay was still a bay.*

- *The first horsecar had yet to come to Boston.*

- *The US consisted of 31 states and 15 territories.*

- *Alaska belonged to Russia.*

Harvey Parker (1805-1884)

WILD ABOUT HARVEY

The concept of "hotel" is a fairly recent one. Hence, in colonial Boston, travelers found rest and refreshment not in hotels or motels, but at local taverns and inns. Since women were rarely on the road, colonial males generally frequented these roadside taverns. They slept in rustic shared bedrooms—and often, shared beds—after spending considerable time quaffing pints of colonial beer. Those taverns were centers for male bonding, conversation, and—in periods of unrest or revolution—secret political meetings.

As these precursors to the modern hotel developed beyond simple taprooms, they began to be known as "houses"—a gentler nomenclature for a far gentler environment. During the second quarter of the nineteenth century, more and more travelers arrived in Boston by coach or ship. Lodging and dining houses proliferated throughout town, many bearing patriotic names, like the American House, the Shawmut, the Adams, and the Revere House. Boston's resident "houses" became so genteel—and sometimes, so luxurious—that even ladies were ably accommodated.

For more than two decades before opening his grand hotel and restaurant on School Street in 1855, Harvey Parker owned and operated an eponymous restaurant at 4 Court Square. Opened in 1832 and couched in a low, dark, and small basement chamber near the old Boston courthouse, "Parker's Restaurant" was where the young entrepreneur developed both the skills and the avid following he would need to prepare for his later grand venture.

Based on this January 25,1850 menu, the original Parker's bill of fare and wine list were admirably varied, but a far cry from the sophisticated French-inspired menu items that Parker and Chef Sanzian would offer in "the white façade that gleams across the way" only a few years later.

In the midst of this period of expansion and change, a twenty-year-old farm boy named Harvey D. Parker arrived in Boston Harbor on a packet boat from Maine. The year was 1825, and his dilemma was real: with less than one dollar in his satchel, young Parker was in immediate need of employment. His first job, as a caretaker for a horse and cow, brought him eight dollars per month. Subsequent work as a coachman for a wealthy Watertown woman garnered somewhat more respectable earnings—and set him on a whole new career path.

Whenever Parker trotted the horse-drawn coach into Boston, the young man ate his noonday meal at a dark cellar cafe on Court Square, owned by one John E. Hunt. By 1832, the ambitious young Parker bought Hunt's cafe for $432 and renamed it Parker's Restaurant. A combination of excellent food and perfect service immediately began attracting a regular clientele of businessmen, lawyers, and newspapermen. By 1847, he took on a partner, John F. Mills. And by 1854, he was ready to embark on a much grander enterprise.

Parker's plan was to build a new, first-class hotel and restaurant at the School Street base of Beacon Hill, just down the road from the domed Massachusetts State House. Despite the competition—especially the popular, modern Tremont House directly across the street—Parker bought the former Mico Mansion on April 22, 1854, and razed the decrepit boarding house. In its place, Parker built an ornate, five-story, Italianate-style stone and brick hotel, faced in gleaming white marble. The first and second floors featured gracefully arched windows, while marble steps led from the sidewalk to the marble foyer within. Once inside, thick carpets and fashionable horse-hair divans completed an air of sumptuous elegance. Above the front door, an engraved sign read simply, "PARKER'S."

Visiting British author Charles Dickens marveled at the splendors of Boston's finest new hotel, in a letter to his daughter:

> *This is an immense hotel, with all manner of white marble public passages and public rooms. I live in a corner, high up, and have a hot and cold bath in my bedroom (connecting with the sitting room) and comforts not in existence when I was here before. The cost of living is enormous, but happily we can afford it.*

Boston's media was also awed by what Parker wrought. A reporter for the *Boston Transcript* fairly raved about the establishment in an October, 1855, review:

This elegant new hotel, on School Street, was opened on Saturday for the inspection of the public. Several thousands of our citizens, ladies as well as gentlemen, availed themselves of the invitation, and for many hours the splendid building was literally thronged. All were surprised and delighted at the convenient arrangement of the whole establishment—the gorgeous furniture of the parlors, the extent and beauty of the dining hall, the number and different styles of the lodging rooms—and, in fact, the richness, lavish expenditure and excellent taste which abounded in every department. The house was universally judged to be a model one.

Inside Harvey Parker

Whenever Harvey D. Parker's name is mentioned, it's invariably in conjunction with the hotel and restaurant he created in 1855 and operated for three decades thereafter. To this day, his Parker House remains an iconic landmark, a preferred destination for historically-minded guests, and the longest continuously operating hotel in the nation.

But what about Parker himself? Who was he? What was his life before 1855? And, outside of his enduring eponymous Boston hotel, how has he been remembered and commemorated since his passing in 1884?

Harvey Drury Parker was born in Temple, Maine, on May 10, 1805. Curiously, that means that Harvey was a native of the Commonwealth of Massachusetts, since Maine was part of the Bay State until 1820. Harvey's hometown of Temple—first settled in 1796, then incorporated in 1803—was a farming town with a robust local economy, thanks to commercial sawmills scattered along the Temple Stream. Temple was a very, very small, and very, very rural village. What is now Maple Street, for example, was once called Cowturd Lane, due to what one source described as "the smell of manure, fresh from cows walking in the road on their way to (pasture) and back, hanging in the air like swamp gas."

Harvey descended from a long line of Parkers who arrived in America around 1635, providing him with a slew of ancestors with names like Hannaniah, Abigail, and Hepsibeth. Harvey's grandfather was among the Minutemen from Westborough, Massachusetts, called to respond to the alarm at Lexington and Concord on April 19, 1775. According to one local story, Grandfather Parker continued fighting in America's War for Independence, serving under one Captain Luke Drury—allegedly the origin of grandson Harvey's middle name. It is more likely that Harvey's middle name came from his mother, Anna Drury.

The quintessential Harvey Parker

The oldest of thirteen children of farmer Pierpont Parker, little Harvey was only seven when his mother Anna died at the age of 34. His father remarried five years later, on October 17, 1817, this time to the widow Sophia Burnham. Federal census records show that Pierpont, Sophia, and their family next settled down in "the prettiest situation in town" in the North End of Andover, Maine. Though the Parkers were recorded as living there in 1820, 1830, and 1840, son Harvey apparently struck out on his own.

By the early 1820s, teenage Harvey was clearly living in Paris, Maine, where he reportedly "mowed and hoed and held the plough" until the age of twenty. Paris, Maine, was known for its scenic beauty, excellent livestock pasturage, rambling apple orchards, and for a founding family named Bisco. Harvey became associated with both the apples and the founding family: he rented a living space in the Bisco district of town, west of the Little Androscoggin River, and—according to a newspaper report found by local historian Ben B. Conant—began his culinary entrepreneurship by vending five-cent apples to folks passing through the bustling Paris courthouse.

Though Harvey spent only a handful of his formative years in Paris, the town remembered him fondly during their Centennial Celebrations of 1879. In the course of those festivities, longtime *Boston Post* editor George F. Emery recited a ten-page poem called "Our Famous Men," which included mention of the then-illustrious Mr. Parker.

The second on this gilded roll,

Whom next we meet while on this stroll,

Though not a native, years ago,

Lived on the farm we call "Bisco."

His name is Parker, Harvey D.,

Whom at the "Hub" you'll often see;

A prince of landlords, hard to beat,

Whose marble halls are on School Street.

In 1825, Harvey left Paris for Portland, Maine, where he hopped a packet and headed for Boston. Though most histories say that Parker snagged an early job as a coachman for "a Watertown woman," a source provided by the Maine Historical Society noted that he also worked for one Dr. George Parkman. If the name rings a bell, it's because the wealthy, Harvard-educated Dr. Parkman was the victim in one of nineteenth century Boston's grisliest crimes: in 1849, Parkman was murdered, chopped into small pieces, and partially burned in a Harvard Med School oven by resident lecturer, John White Webster. Whether Harvey Parker was or was not once employed by George Parkman, however, is moot insofar as the latter's gruesome fate: the murder took place more than two decades after the alleged employment would have occurred.

The 1830s featured two milestone events in Harvey's life. In 1832, he used his savings to purchase Hunt's Restaurant, a small basement cafe at 4 Court Street, on the corner of Court Street and Court Avenue, by the old Boston Courthouse. It was there where he learned the ropes, sharpened his entrepreneurial skills, and developed a following of fans that adored both his food and service. The second Parker milestone of the decade was on Thanksgiving Day, 1839, when he married Julia Ann Brown, daughter of Joseph and Suzannah Brown, at the family's grand house on 25 Cass Street, Exeter, New Hampshire.

Julia has occasionally been credited as the creator of the Parker House Roll. She certainly took an administrative role in running the Parker House, but it's not entirely clear whether she was doing any baking. Moreover, a mysterious man always referred to as "a German baker named Ward" is traditionally credited for the famed fluffy rolls, most likely in the 1870s. What Julia Parker *did* do is help her husband build up the business that made the Parker House roll a staple today.

During the thirty years he spent perfecting the Parker House, Harvey Parker was known for making friends, aquiring followers, caring for his extended family, and striving for excellence. It's virtually impossible to find any recorded complaints about him or any defamation of his character. Parker regularly walked about the hotel dining room at mealtimes, smiling at and chatting with his guests. He would often sit down with them at table, particularly if they were friends like Charles Levi Woodbury, lawyer Charles Donnelly, or grand opera star, Clara Louise Kellogg (who always had the choicest third floor suite when performing in Boston).

Internationally-acclaimed opera star, Clara Louise Kellogg, was one of Harvey Parker's favorite guests; she was also among those who ignored the "no-flowers" request at Parker's funeral. This portrait was taken between 1855 and 1865.

In a 1925 newspaper interview, longtime employee Michael Maynes remembered Harvey's popularity amongst the staff as well. "His waiters used to agree that Mr. Parker was incapable of being unjust to anyone. I don't believe he was ever known to be angry." Maynes traveled from Ireland in 1871 to take a job at the Parker House, and recalled that although Harvey hired a variety of nationalities, "he preferred Irishmen to all others.... and the headwaiters were invariably Irish."

Recent research unearthed only two vaguely negative references to Harvey over the past century and a half. From the time he first opened his doors, Parker's bars were well-known hangouts for the Harvard student body—with its equally well-known penchant for alcoholic consumption. Appreciating this regular clientele, Harvey was known to lock those doors when he saw North End gangs coming to his cellar restaurant "in hope of provoking a fight there with Harvard students." Parker also reportedly disliked the gloomy old stone church that faced Parker's on School Street—

the ancient and honorable King's Chapel. A captain named James Codman claimed Harvey once told him, "I wish they'd pull down that old King's Chapel opposite. Such kind of buildings aren't no use in these times."

If Parker did ever make such a Philistinic remark, he more than atoned for his sins in his will: Harvey left $100,000 to the new Museum of Fine Arts in Boston, which became the foundation of its modern print department (*see story on page 88*).

Throughout his decades of critical commercial and culinary success, Parker supported his father and stepmother and provided for all his brothers and sisters. He was eventually able to convince his parents to move to Boston, setting them up in a comfortable home in nearby Chelsea. Though Parker reportedly dreamed of passing his business on to a long line of descendants, that was not meant to be. Harvey and Julia had two sons, Theodore and Hayward. Little Theodore died at the age of seven, in 1850. Fifteen years later, Harvey sent 24-year Hayward, his oldest son and heir apparent, to China on the ship *Eagle Wing*, a clipper built by James O. Curtis of nearby Medford. The ship, his son, and his dreams were lost at sea in 1865, leaving Harvey heartbroken.

Harvey Parker himself lived to the age of 79, dying in his home at 141 Boylston Street on May 31, 1884. Boston newspapers gave profuse and compassionate coverage to his funeral services, first held privately at home, followed by a public service at the Arlington Street Church, on the corner of Arlington and Boylston streets. The esteemed Unitarian divine, Reverend Minot J. Savage, presided over the event. "The hand of death is here," began the coverage in the *Boston Globe*. The reporter noted that the façade of the Parker House was heavily draped in mourning, since its "kindly-hearted proprietor was sleeping his last sleep." Meanwhile, business went on, but not as usual, at Harvey's old hotel. Parker House staff spoke in whispers, and seemed to move at a slower pace than usual, reflecting the solemnity of the occasion.

Though a request had been published asking that no flowers be sent, the world seemingly ignored that entreaty. Among the most elegant floral displays at the Arlington Street Church were arrangements given by the Boston Club—of which Harvey was an honored member—as well as by the Waiter's Benevolent Association, Chicago's Grand Pacific Hotel, the Windsor Hotel of Montreal, the Revere House in Boston, Miss Clara Louise Kellogg, and both the clerks and the cooks of the Parker House.

Since Harvey had no living children, his will provided for his nieces and nephews—as well as for his wife Julia (who outlived him by eleven years), the Museum of Fine Arts, Boston, and outstanding debts of the Parker House. Like many of his wealthy, famous, and influential Boston peers, Harvey had purchased a burial lot for his extended family at Mount Auburn Cemetery, on the Cambridge-Watertown line. The centerpiece and most prominent monument in the 600 square foot curbed lot, set in the Laurel Hill section of the cemetery, is a cenotaph honoring his son who died at sea. Harvey's own last resting place is marked by a scroll-topped stone, decorated with a carved cross and strand of laurel, reading simply, "In Memory of Harvey D. Parker."

Harvey and his extended family are buried in a curbed lot, number 3334, on Laurel Hill, Mount Auburn Cemetery.

FOOD FOR THOUGHT

Harvey Parker's earlier experience with Parker's Restaurant had taught him that catering to the local crowd—providing Bostonians with a fine and flexible dining experience—was equally important to his business as offering visitors architecturally elegant lodgings. Hence, in a day when a good Boston cook could be hired for eight dollars per week, or $416 a year, Parker hired the gourmet French chef Sanzian (spelled Sanizan by some sources) for an astonishing annual salary of $5,000.

Sanzian's versatile menu drew large crowds and ongoing accolades. A typical Parker's banquet of the 1850s or '60s might include green turtle soup, ham in champagne sauce, aspic of oysters, filet of beef with mushrooms, mongrel goose, black-breast plover, charlotte russe, mince pie, and a variety of fruits, nuts, and ice creams. Among Sanzian's specialities were tomato soup, venison-chop sauce, and delicate mayonnaise, plus a distinctive method of roasting beef and fowl using a revolving spit over well-stoked coals.

From a creative point of view, Parker's was not only the best; it was frequently the first as well. Boston Cream Pie and lemon meringue pie, for example, were perfected and popularized in nineteenth-century Parker House kitchens. The Boston Cream Pie story in particular is an interesting one.

When the Parker House opened in 1855, chocolate was mainly consumed at home as a beverage or in puddings. (There was no lack of chocolate in Boston, since America's first chocolate mill had opened in neighboring Dorchester back in 1765.) Since colonial times, New Englanders had enjoyed a dessert called American "Pudding-cake pie"—of which Boston Cream Pie is a direct descendant. But when Chef Sanzian's bake staff drizzled chocolate icing onto sponge cake filled with vanilla custard, something new and sensational was born. Originally dubbed "Chocolate Cream Pie" or "Parker House Chocolate Cream Pie," Boston Cream Pie became an immediate, and a perennial, hit.

The original Parker House recipe for the pie (which is technically a cake) was so popular that in 1958 it became a Betty Crocker boxed mix. On December 12, 1996, thanks in part to a Norton High School civics class that sponsored the bill, Boston Cream Pie was proclaimed the official Massachusetts State Dessert. The bill was signed into law, of course, in the Omni Parker House Press Room. Among the pie's stiff competitors were the Toll House Cookie, the Fig Newton, and Indian Pudding.

The most recent Boston Cream Pie episode came during the Omni Parker House's gala 150th anniversary celebrations. In the fall of 2005, the World's Largest Boston Cream Pie was displayed at historic Fanueil Hall Marketplace. Sixteen feet in diameter, and topped with another Boston Cream Pie resembling the Parker House in 1855, the monstrous dessert included 1,300 pounds of cake, 800 pounds of filling, and 500 pounds of chocolate frosting. Though the total caloric value was more than two million calories, those calories were divided among an estimated 6,750 people.

The Mayor's Office declared October 8, 2005, to be Omni Parker House 150th Anniversary Day: "The City of Boston extends its deepest congratulations to the Omni Parker House Hotel on the auspicious occasion of its 150th anniversary and for the honor of being America's longest continuously operating hotel …"

Parker House Rolls

Yield: 2 dozen rolls

Ingredients

1/2 cup scalded milk
1/2 cup boiling water
1 tsp. salt
1 tsp. sugar
1 tbsp. butter
1/2 yeast cake dissolved in 1/4 cup lukewarm water
3 cups bread flour, or enough to knead

Method

Place milk, water, salt, butter and sugar into mixing bowl and mix well. Add yeast. Then add flour until it is stiff enough to knead. Cover and let it rise to double its bulk, shape into balls, put into buttered pan and cover. Let it rise in a warm place again to double its bulk. With the floured handle of a wooden spoon press the balls through the center, almost cutting in half. Brush one half with butter, fold the other half over and press together like a pocketbook. Let it rise again and bake in a hot oven (400° F) for 15 minutes. Brush the tops with butter after baking.

The moist, fluffy, and internationally known Parker House Roll was the inspired creation of an in-house German baker named Ward, who worked under Chef John Bonello. For many decades in the nineteenth and twentieth centuries, the famed rolls were packaged and shipped from the kitchens here to hotels, restaurants, and stores across the U.S. Today, they are still served to Omni Parker House guests—and imitated everywhere. The rolls' precise ingredients, incidentally, remained a well-kept secret until 1933, when, according to legend, Franklin and Eleanor Roosevelt requested the recipe be forwarded to them in Washington (*see story on page 28*).

Legend has it that the term scrod also originated at Parker's. Though many disagree over its precise definition, the word is generally used for cod or other white-fleshed fish that are the youngest, freshest, smallest, or best of the day's catch. Unlike cod, haddock, or halibut, scrod is not a type of fish.

As plentiful and interesting as the food found in Parker's restaurant were the spirits served in its bars. Early menus list such interesting concoctions as Sherry Cobbler,

PARKER'S RESTAURANT
NO. 4, COURT SQUARE, BOSTON.

Timber Doodle, Mint Julep, Gin Sling, Sangaree, and the "Cocktail." More conventional draughts of rum, whiskey, and gin were also always available, as were fine wines. As might be expected, single men were regulars in the barroom. And though all bars attract the occasional rowdy, Parker's hosted a hefty dose of merchants, businessmen, writers, politicians, and philosophers. Harvard students readily found their way across the Charles River or wandered in from the nearby medical school, inspiring humorist Artemus Ward to note, "[Harvard College], this celebrated institootion of learnin' is pleasantly situated in the Bar-room of Parker's, in Scool street…"

Another culinary innovation initiated under Harvey Parker, known as the "European Plan," separated the charges for food and lodging. Before the mid-nineteenth century, American inns and hotels generally lumped room and board together in a single fee; this so-called "American Plan" was a thrifty meal service that often resulted in rigid dining schedules and uninspired, mass-produced, and quite ordinary meals. When Parker's became the first hotel in Boston to employ the European Plan, they made á la carte food available to guests any time of the day or evening. While the system allowed lodgers more flexibility, it also gave Parker's staff the time to select, develop, perfect, and personalize their varied dishes—a deliciously radical departure from hotel dining convention.

To this day, the Omni Parker House offers guests superb culinary creations and exceptional personal service. Parker's menus, meanwhile, continue to balance what we now consider traditional New England fare—from Parker House Rolls, Boston Cream Pie, and Baked Boston Scrod to New England Clam Chowder and Pan Seared Jonah Crab Cakes—with eclectic continental cuisine.

ROOM AND BOARD

Many Americans are used to requesting "room and board," but few stop to think what that phrase really means. In colonial times, the family dining table was called a board because that's what it was—a big, long, wide, wooden board. As a result, the expression "room and board" meant a room to sleep in and a board to eat on. Generally, the family would sit on a long common bench along the side of the board, while the father sat at the end in a chair. And yes, that was the origin of "chair-man of the board."

Mrs. Roosevelt and the Rolls

On November 12, 1941, Henrietta Nesbitt, Eleanor Roosevelt, and Harriet Elliott met at the White House to sign a pledge to spend wisely and conserve.

An urban legend about Eleanor Roosevelt and her love for Parker House Rolls has circulated for decades. The scenario runs generally like this:

> *The exact recipe for Parker House rolls was a well-kept secret until one day in 1933, when the First Lady of the United States requested a copy. Once Mrs. Roosevelt received the recipe, the genie was out of the bottle—or, in this instance, out of the Parker House baking pan.*

It's a great tale—but is it true? In an effort to separate fact from fiction, we began researching with the aid of two amazing facilities—the Arthur and Elizabeth Schlesinger Library on the History of Women in America (Cambridge, Massachusetts) and the Franklin D. Roosevelt Presidential Library and Museum (Hyde Park, New York).

The results were fascinating—though not exactly definitive.

There is no question that Eleanor Roosevelt was drawn to American cooking and cooking history. Her mind frequently ran to the topic of food, though she herself apparently ate very little.

While husband Franklin was governor of New York, the couple lived in Hyde Park, New York. There they met Henrietta Nesbitt, a neighbor who was locally famous for her baked goods. During the period when Franklin was running for governor, Mrs. Roosevelt asked if she could pay Mrs. Nesbitt to cook for Roosevelt campaign parties and events. Nesbitt agreed and soon discovered that baking all her local specialties for the Roosevelts—from pies, cakes, and cookies to rolls, strudels, and streusels—was an excellent way to pay the rent.

Fast forward to FDR's election to the Presidency.

Portrait of Franklin Delano Roosevelt

When Eleanor and Franklin moved to the White House in March of 1933, Eleanor asked Mrs. Nesbitt to join her and become First Housekeeper of the land. Though Nesbitt was on the verge of her fifty-ninth birthday, she and her husband uprooted and began the jobs of their lifetime: she, as Mrs. Roosevelt's housekeeper and head cook and he, as White House custodian and steward. "Mrs. Roosevelt and I always found a lot to talk about," remembered Nesbitt in her book, White House Diary. "We talked a lot about cooking and in a way it was a loaf of bread that sent me to the White House with the Roosevelts."

As Nesbitt recalled, the White House kitchen was a mess when they moved in (one news-paperman compared it to "an old-fashioned German Rathskeller"). For starters, there was the bad-smelling icebox with a wooden interior (the precursor of the modern refrigerator), not to mention sinks with badly worn wooden drainpipes and a room filled with dangerously old wiring. But more than being dirty, dismal, and outdated, the White House kitchen didn't have a single cookbook. As a result, Mrs. Nesbitt, who had collected cookbooks and recipes all her life, had to start from scratch with her own resources.

And that's where the Parker House Roll story kicks in.

Working the White House kitchen for a total of thirteen years—twelve for the Roosevelts and one with the Trumans—Mrs. Nesbitt planned menus for thousands of meals and thousands of guests. She oversaw suppers for everyone from Franklin's old Harvard pals and members of the Hasty Pudding Club to Winston Churchill, Will Rogers, General Douglas McArthur, and a bevy of British monarchs.

During Nesbitt's tenure, there was one item that consistently graced the dinner table: fresh-baked bread in one format or another, including rolls. "There is nothing on earth equal to the smell of fresh bread…," she acknowledged in her published diary. And nothing, apparently, like Parker House Rolls, a recipe for which appeared on page 148 of Nesbitt's second book, *The Presidential Cookbook: Feeding the Roosevelts and Their Guests.*

The remaining question, of course, is just how did Helen Nesbitt get the recipe for Parker House rolls that she baked in the Roosevelt

kitchen, placed in the White House cookbook, and published in her own memoirs? Research into the vast collections of correspondence held by the Franklin D. Roosevelt Presidential Library in Hyde Park failed to unearth a single letter to or from Eleanor or Helen and Parker House staff. But the request for the secret recipe and the Parker House response may well have been executed in person rather than in writing, since Franklin and Eleanor were frequent visitors to both Boston and the Parker House. FDR was not only a Harvard alum, but also a close colleague of James Michael Curley—who was an avid supporter of Roosevelt's presidential campaign, a frequent Mayor of Boston, and a constant frequenter of the Parker House.

So is the urban legend about Mrs. Roosevelt and the rolls true? Based on circumstantial evidence, we propose that the answer is, Yes…. probably!

Henrietta Nesbitt's The Presidential Cookbook: Feeding the Roosevelts and Their Guests, *was published by Doubleday in 1951. Nesbitt's version of the Parker House Roll recipe appeared on page 148.*

Offenbach on a Roll

Despite his successes, he was near bankruptcy in 1874, so planned an American concert tour to help regain his solvency. Curiously, a simple stay at the Parker House during his 1876 U.S. tour lit a spark that inspired Offenbach to write not another operetta, but an opera—and the masterpiece for which he is best known.

During his first dinner in Parker's Restaurant, the composer was served soft, crustless Parker House Rolls, which delighted him to no end. He initially hummed a tune in their praise, then began singing, "Parker rolls, Parker rolls, how I love you," to the amusement of the other diners.

German-born French composer Jacques Offenbach (1819-1880)—shown here in a portrait by famed French photographer Félix Nadar—composed nearly one hundred operettas and helped elevate that form to a bona fide genre on theatrical stages.

Later, Offenbach enlarged on this theme and created his only full-fledged opera, Les Contes d'Hoffmann ("The Tales of Hoffmann"). Though Offenbach died before the opera was completed, his son and a family friend finished it and brought it to the stage several months after the composer's death.

Malcolm X, then known as Malcolm Little, was a busboy at the Parker House during the time of the Pearl Harbor invasion.

In the nineteenth century, Harvey Parker and his successors ensured the excellence of the Parker's dining experience by hiring European chefs like Sanzian and Bonello. In the twentieth and twenty-first centuries, that tradition continued with talents such as longtime Parker's chef Joseph Ribas and a slew of rising restaurant stars—including Jasper White, Lydia Shire, Emeril Lagasse, and Paul O'Connell—who directed or creatively cooked in Parker's kitchens while sharpening their culinary crafts.

It's interesting to note that talent and fame were not restricted to the European and American chefs who graced the Parker House kitchens. Two cultural icons and notable revolutionaries spent time on the Parker House staff: Vietnamese leader Ho Chi Minh served as a baker in the bakeshop from 1912 to 1913, and Malcolm Little—remembered as black activist, Malcolm X—was a busboy in the early 1940s, during the period of the Pearl Harbor invasion. In the mid-1980s, a student at the New England Conservatory of Music was also employed at the Omni Parker House, as a night-shift telephone operator. Today, she is best known as mezzo-soprano opera star, Denyce Graves.

Dutchess Divider

Although most of the work involved in making Parker House Rolls is done strictly by hand, one machine is considered essential to the process. After the dough is mixed and kneaded, this sturdy old Dutchess Divider is used to press down and cut that dough into equal portions. Finally, the rolls are pulled out and individually folded on a large baking sheet. How long has this been going on at the Omni Parker House? Pretty much forever.

Parker House
Boston

Dinner,   Sunday, Dec. 28, '02

	Blue Points, per dozen	50		Little Neck Clams, per dozen	40
Relishes.	Celery	30	Oscar's Sauce	15	Stuffed Olives	25	Radishes	15
Soups.	Mock Turtle			Consommé, Plain	30
	Green Turtle			Consommé, Légumes	30
	Clear Green Tur...		of Beef à la Russe	60
Fish.	Boil...	half portion	40
	Baked Oysters i...		60
	Smelts Sautée, ...	gues and Pork	40
	Filet of Haddoc...		60
		50
		65
Boiled.	Chicken, half, C...	...Cabbage	50
Roast.	Sirloin of Beef		75
	Young Turkey, ...	...half	75
	Chicken, half		60
Entrees.	Terrapin à la Ma...
	Lamb Cutlets à l...
	Lobster Patties,
	Fil...
Game.	Broiled Black D...
	Broiled Venison
Vegetables.	Boil...

DINNER
FOR
Sixteen Gentlemen
AT
THE PARKER HOUSE
JANUARY 8TH,
1856.

KING'S CHAPEL IN 1870

PARKER HOUSE
School and Tremont Streets, Boston, Mass.

REVERE ROOM
Parker House
SCHOOL and TREMONT STREETS
BOSTON MASS.

Cold D...				50
				50
				50
Salads.			on	25
				1 00
				50
				60
Puddings.		Banana ...	25
Dessert.		Vanilla Eclairs	15	Blanc ...	25
		Angel Cake	15	Bowl Custard	15
		Charlotte Russe	25	Dark Fruit Cake	15
		French Kisses	15	Coffee Jelly with Cream	20
		15	Sponge Drops and Fingers	15
Cheese.		Brie	25	Cream	20
Ices.		...laret Sauce	25	Méringue à la Panaché	25
		...am	25	Tutti Frutti	25
		...Sherbet	25	Coffee Ice Cream	25
		...n 25	Vanilla Ice Cream 25	Frozen Pudding, Whipped Cream	30
		Any Plain Ice Cream, half portion	15
Fru...	Malaga Grapes	35	Apples	20	Oranges	25
	Beurre Bosc Pears	25	Catawba Grapes	25	Bananas	20
			Grape Fruit, half	25
Tea,	Pot of Tea	20	Cup of Coffee	10	Chocolate	25
Coffee, etc.	Small Pot of Tea	15	Coffee, Pot	20	Broma	25	Cocoa	25
	Café Noir, Demi Tasse	10	Small Pot of Coffee	15	Horlick's Malted Milk	

Culinary Stars, Then and Now

For decades, the story has been passed down that legendary North Vietnamese leader Ho Chi Minh (1890–1969) was once employed at the Parker House. Current scholarship suggests that the tale is actually true, though the facts, like Ho himself, are still shrouded in mystery.

As a young man, Nguyen Sinh Cung was forced to leave his homeland of French Indochina—and to assume a variety of pseudonyms and disguises—in order to avoid arrest for his anti-colonialist, pro-Communist activities. The itinerant expatriate worked a variety of odd jobs, spending several years at sea, working in the kitchens of steamships, and making stops in various African and Asian countries, as well as France, England, and the United States.

During a stateside sojourn of several months in 1912 and 1913, Ho (then called Nguyen Tat Thanh, or simply Ba) spent time in New York City, the Southern States, and Boston, where he worked as a cook's helper and pastry chef in the Parker House. Ho apparently had culinary talent and later apprenticed with the famed chef Auguste Escoffier at the Carlton Hotel. His baking skills, however, were simply a sideline to his life mission of freeing his country from French rule and promoting the international Communist movement.

In the summer of 2005, a Vietnamese delegation that included Prime Minister Phan Van Khai and Truong Quang Duoc, Vice President of the National Assembly, visited the Omni Parker House to view the hotel and basement pastry kitchen where Ho once worked. The marble table the future Vietnamese leader baked on is still there and is actively used to this day.

33

Celebrity chef Emeril Lagasse is one of the many TV food stars—including Martha Stewart, Bobby Flay, and Beau MacMillan—who have broadcast shows in or about the Parker House, featuring their respective takes on classic Parker House Rolls, Boston Scrod, or Boston Cream Pie.

For Lagasse, however, the Omni Parker House is more than a tasty tourist destination; it's also his old stomping grounds. From 1979 to 1981 he served as Sous Chef in the Parker kitchens. Among his fondest memories was the night a guest called him to the table to compliment him on his work. To his delight, the complimentary customer was none other than Julia Child.

It took some time for Lagasse to become the megawatt personality and internationally-known restaurateur he is today. This 1979 clip from the Parker House staff newsletter suggests that it wasn't even clear how young Emeril spelled his first name!

In the kitchen, Emero LaGasse has been named the new Junior Sous Chef from Chef Tournant. LaGasse was also Chef Tournant at the Berkshire Place before coming to the Parker House.

The Farm that Fed the Parker House

Seven years after Harvey Parker's death, another culinary innovator took the helm at the Parker House. His name was J. Reed Whipple and his fame came, in part, from the unique contribution he made to the Parker House food chain. Whipple literally "bought the farm" and brought its fresh produce to Parker House tables for more than two decades. Here is Whipple's story.

In the early years of the twentieth century, when Parker House guests requested an order of milk, cream, or buttermilk, they would be served glass bottles with embossed metal caps reading, "J.R. Whipple Co. Dairy, New Boston, N.H."

Though a simple bottle cap may seem unimpressive at first glance, it turns out that dairy owner J. Reed Whipple—called simply "Reed" by his friends—was one of the most successful American businessmen of his era. The New Hampshire-born Whipple not only owned the dairy that bore his name and embossed his bottle caps, but also presided over the sprawling 2,500-acre Valley View Farm in the little village of New Boston. Meanwhile, back in "old" Boston, Reed was heralded as the wealthy CEO of the Whipple Company, which managed three of the Hub's prime commercial properties: the Parker House, the Hotel Touraine, and Young's Hotel.

And therein lies quite a story.

J. Reed Whipple left his family farm and home in New Boston, New Hampshire, initially to work as a grocer in Roxbury, Massachusetts. His finest move was gaining employment as a second-assistant steward at the Parker House, where young Whipple became inspired by Harvey Parker's masterful touch. Though Whipple left Parker's employ after eleven years, his hard work, talent, and shrewd business planning led him to form a partnership, eventually taking over management of Young's (1876) and building the Touraine (1902). On May 15, 1891, Whipple assumed control of the Parker House as well.

In order to provide his Boston diners with the freshest and finest food products available, the hotelier and his Whipple Company established its own 2,500-acre dairy farm in 1881, set on the banks of the Piscataquog River in his old home turf of New Boston, New Hampshire. Whipple's Valley View Farm was divided into three departments: the Dairy took care of milking cows, producing milk, and making butter; the Piggery bred and cared for pigs, which were then slaughtered and shipped to Boston; and in the Hennery, chickens were raised and eggs laid. Some ninety people were employed between these three departments.

Catering to the Dairy, Piggery, and Hennery was the Farming Department, which provided feed for all the stock and for thirty work horses, while maintaining thirty-five wagons for use throughout the farm. Hay, fodder corn, and apples from the plentiful orchards set on the rolling hills above the farmhouse were all used as part of this largely self-contained farming production.

In 1893, in order to supply his hotels with all these fresh products, J.R. Whipple helped build a railroad depot in New Boston, connecting the existing main lines with a spur track that was later leased to the Boston & Maine. As a result, it was not only New Boston Creamery milk and butter that was delivered daily to the Parker House. Twice a day, Whipple's trains traveled from New Boston to old Boston, carting dairy products along with fresh beef, sausage, bacon, pork, ham, poultry, eggs, apples, apple cider vinegar—and even freshly washed and ironed linens for use in his hotels.

"When the trains came back from Boston, they would bring back wooden barrels with sealed covers with garbage and pastry from the hotels," recalled New Boston native son Oliver H. Dodge in a 1991 interview. "Some of the barrels contained nothing but pastry and cakes that weren't touched. The help could take what they wanted and it was said that sometimes more was consumed by the two legged pigs than the four legged ones. These barrels were then dumped out to feed the pigs."

For almost three decades, Whipple's enterprise grew and flourished. In 1910, the J.R. Whipple company published a lavishly illustrated, 80-page, hard-bound book entitled About the Farm, which heralded the great successes of Valley View. Less than two years later, Whipple died at age 69, following an operation for stomach trouble performed at the Elliot Hospital, at 107 Audubon Road in Boston's Back Bay (According to the New York Times obituary, the specific ailment was cancer of the stomach).

After Whipple's death, his son-in-law Edgar Pierce ran both Valley View Farm and the Boston hotels. Brothers Fred and Daniel Gilman of St. Johnsbury, Vermont, bought the farm from Pierce on October 19, 1919. After running Valley View on a substantially smaller scale for less than two years, the Gilmans held a three-day auction for the site and all its trappings in May, 1921. Little by little, Valley View's component parts were sold off—a barn, farmhouse, or creamery here, an orchard, farm machine, heads of cattle or herds of pigs there.

Today, visitors to New Boston can still see remnants of Mr. Whipple's glory days at Valley View Farm, thanks to conscious community preservation, creative re-use of old structures, and the work of the New Boston Historical Society. The Society's home is in the Wason Memorial Building, the old library that once contained J.R. Whipple's collection of books. That book collection was graciously gifted to the village by the entrepreneur's wife, Rose Higgins Whipple, following her husband's death.

35

THE FARMHOUSE, THEN & NOW

The bright, yellow, ten-room residential farmhouse at Valley View Farm sat on a hillside at the junction of today's Routes 77 and 136. The large structure shown behind the farmhouse in the early photo was a horse stable and piggery. Though the barn burned on March 31, 1930, two stone posts behind the house still show the old entranceway.

COWS & MILK PRODUCTS

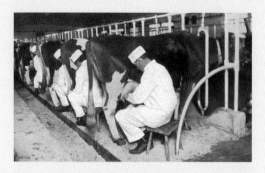

At its height, J.R. Whipple's Valley View Farms boasted a herd of 350 cattle, both Holsteins and Guernseys. When not out to pasture, the cows lived in a widely-publicized, state-of-the-art, $100,000 "Cement Barn" that Whipple built especially for this purpose. The cows were hand-milked year round, at 3:30 a.m. and 3:30 p.m., with a good milker averaging ten to fifteen cows per hour.

Despite the large herds, Whipple's farm needed additional milk to supply his Boston hotels. As a result, he bought milk and cream from neighboring New Boston area farmers and paid them based on the percentage of butter fat. Part of the milk produced was bottled for table use at Whipple's Boston hotels, while the rest was delivered in the form of cooking milk, cream, and butter.

THE CEMENT BARN, THEN & NOW

New Bostonian Oliver H. Dodge fondly remembered the Cement Barn in a 1991 interview. His tale focused on a banquet held for its grand opening. "They had some big celebrations in the Cement Barn, the men all tell. When they dedicated it, they brought all the help up from the hotels in Boston. They set tables up the whole length of the cow barns, had waiters and a 100 foot table in the middle of the hay barn. They had a bar set up and everyone was invited. The local people had never had cocktails before. It was said that many a man didn't make it home for chores that night."

The Creamery, Then & Now

After being carried from the new cement barn to the milk room, where it was weighed and annotated, the milk traveled by wagon to the modern, sterile New Boston Creamery for cooling and bottling. The fresh milk was carted in embossed milk pails, specially designed and fabricated for the operation.

Set on the banks of the Piscataquog River in a little park of elms, shrubs, and grasses, the Creamery once produced 2,000 quarts of cream, 6,000 quarts of milk, and four tons of butter per month. The Creamery building, now used for private apartments, still stands behind Dodge's Store and the Apple Barn.

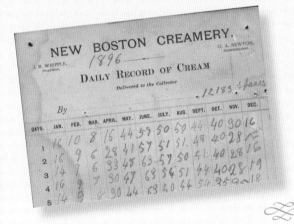

The Creamery Record

On the top right corner of this 1896 Creamery Record are the words "12183 spaces." A space was a unit of measure in the late 1800s. The delivering farmer was paid according to the number of "spaces" of cream collected by the driver, who was an employee of the factory.

Horses & Wagons

Before tractors were in common use, thirty Valley View horses were used to plow and pull the wagons, sometimes using wheeled carts and sometimes hauling sleighs.

Apple Orchards & Cider Vinegar

Today, housing developments stretch across the hills above New Boston, sitting amidst a few scattered apple trees. These acres were once covered by Valley View Farm orchards, which provided apples and pure cider vinegar for the Whipple Corporation. The old cider mill structure, now a private home, housed a mill and a cider press run by a gasoline engine. In the concrete basement below, cider was stored in barrels for two years, then turned into large vats for a third year, before shipping out to Boston as vinegar.

The Piggery

Valley View's piggery building and pastures covered forty acres of the farm. A century ago, there were sometimes as many as 1800 Yorkshires on site. Inside the piggery, the pigs drank skim milk from iron feeding troughs, siphoned from the dairy via iron pipes. Once a pig reached 175 pounds, it was sent to the slaughterhouse. Dressed pigs were packed into farm-owned refrigerator cars and shipped to the Parker House, where they were cut up and distributed to Whipple's three hotels as sausage, bacon, pork, and ham.

THE ICE POND

Before the advent of refrigeration, ice blocks were harvested by farmers in the winter, then stored for use in year-round cooling. In order to supply the cooling necessary to run his dairy business, J.R. Whipple built his own artificial Ice Pond on River Road, by the entrance to what is now called the New Boston Fairgrounds.

Fed by a brook on a nearby hill, the Ice Pond froze over during the long New Hampshire winter. Crews of men, sometimes alone and sometimes with horse ploughs, cut long slabs from the sheets of ice, raised them up to a platform using a simple elevator, then chopped and slid the ice cakes into three ice houses at pond's edge. While most of the ice was used in

New Boston, some of the cakes were also used for refrigerator cars on Whipple's trains.

Before harvesting began, local kids would skate on the pond every night, warmed and lighted by a backyard bonfire.

RAILROAD DEPOT & THE TRAIN, THEN & NOW

Twice a day, trains would travel between Boston and New Boston, terminating at the depot built by J.R. Whipple. Before Whipple's time, train service from Boston ended at Parker Station in Goffstown. Whipple

helped extend the rail line almost six miles, which joined New Boston to the rest of the world. The depot is now a private home, and the old railroad right-of-way a hiking path.

J.R. Whipple died in 1912. His farm was auctioned off in 1921.

WEDDING SHOOTS AT THE PARKER HOUSE

Boston's award-winning photographers, Jill Person and Laurén Killian, have photographed weddings at the Omni Parker House since the duo's first year of business, in 2004.

"We love shooting at the Omni Parker," explains Person. "When you enter the lobby—with the heavy chandeliers, the dark wood—it's obvious that it has by the far the most old world charm anywhere in Boston. Couples who book their weddings here are really into that—Old Boston, Old World. You could open your eyes and it could be one hundred years ago!"

Person+Killian's favorite photo spots include many of the most picturesque sites in or near the Omni Parker House. Couples and groups are posed and captured in action near the lobby chandeliers, by the gleaming brass elevator doors, under the theatrical marquis at the School Street entrance, or in front of Old City Hall, a well-preserved 1865 building which has been compared in appearance to a multi-layered wedding cake.

"The Omni Parker House and School Street have an aura about them," adds Person. "It's an artistic setting. It's unique. And it's fun!"

Though a variety of rooms are available for wedding events, the mezzanine-level Press Room—where John F. Kennedy famously declared his first run for Congress in 1946—is a favorite spot for ceremonies. The old Rooftop Ballroom was added in 1935, to the delight of Bostonians seeking the ultimate aerial view of the city. Today that ballroom proves a perfect space for parties, dancing, and music into the wee hours.

GUESS WHO'S
COMING TO DINNER?

Harvey Parker's commitment to superior service, fair prices, fine food and drink, and handsome surroundings drew legions of guests into his hotel's restaurants and bars. Equally vital to his bustling restaurant business, however, was the hotel's ideal downtown location—which all but guaranteed Parker's a clientele that included poets, philosophers, politicians, and performers.

The Tremont Theatre, which hosted literary, musical, and political events, made its debut around the corner from the future Parker House site in 1828. Horticultural Hall, home of the powerful Massachusetts Horticultural Society, was built next door to Parker's site in 1844. The Boston Athenaeum, a prestigious, well-stocked, membership library, opened its fine new home one block away, on Beacon Street, in 1849. Meanwhile, King's Chapel—Boston's first Anglican Church and, later, America's first Unitarian church—remained a popular and perennial draw to worshippers and visitors alike. And two of the town's most historic burying grounds, King's Chapel and the Granary, were located but a heartbeat away. (These old graveyards regularly attracted friends and families of the deceased, as well as pilgrims fascinated

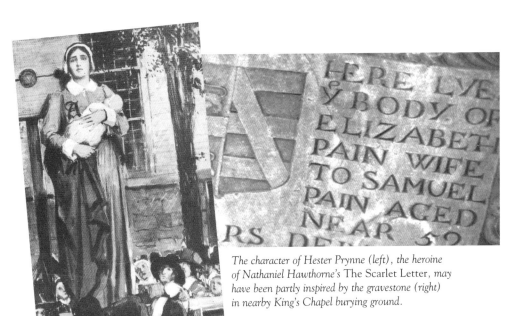

The character of Hester Prynne (left), the heroine of Nathaniel Hawthorne's The Scarlet Letter, *may have been partly inspired by the gravestone (right) in nearby King's Chapel burying ground.*

by funerary art and the final resting places of celebrities like John Winthrop, Paul Revere, John Hancock, "Mother Goose," and the parents of Ben Franklin.)

There were two Boston buildings in particular, however, that proved most vital to the international fame and ongoing success of the 1855 Parker House. One was Boston's French Empire-style City Hall, which opened its doors across the street from Parker's in 1865. A second was the Old Corner Bookstore. Built as the apothecary shop of Thomas Crease in 1718, the quaint brick structure gained international renown from 1829 to 1903, when it housed a series of ten bookselling and publishing firms—and created a matching "bookend" with the Athenaeum up the street.

BOSTON AT 300

General Edward Lawrence Logan, an esteemed war veteran and organizer of the Massachusetts National Guard, was Chief Marshall of the parade. Logan is best remembered today as the namesake of Boston's international airport.

At the start of the Great Depression, The Hub needed to find—and did find—something to celebrate. September 17, 1930 was the three hundredth anniversary of the founding of Boston. For many months prior, a committee of eight hundred men and women met regularly at City Hall planning "Boston Week," "Boston Day," and a variety of special exhibits, talks, and activities to commemorate Boston's tercentennial. Though Wednesday the 17th was apparently a drizzly September day, the mammoth "Boston Day Parade" was touted as "a procession of impressive length and astonishing beauty," and served as both the climax and standout event of the commemorative festivities.

This photo, taken from an upper floor of the Parker House, shows the front courtyard of Boston's Old City Hall and celebratory British and American flags hanging from the Parker House. More than a million onlookers came out to enjoy a parade that lasted from high noon until past sunset.

LITERARY LIAISONS

The most illustrious group to call the Parker House home was certainly that nineteenth-century men's social gathering known as the Saturday Club. A hint at the caliber of the club's membership is alluded to in an 1867 letter from visiting British author, Charles Dickens:

I dine today with Longfellow, Emerson, Holmes, and Agassiz.
Longfellow was here yesterday. Perfectly white in hair and beard,
but a remarkably handsome and notable-looking man.

Why did some of the finest minds in nineteenth-century Boston choose to hold their monthly meetings at Parker's? Location was not the only factor—though it certainly was an essential one.

Up the street, as noted earlier, was the Boston Athenaeum. Incorporated in 1807 as a private reading room, library, and art museum, the Athenaeum became a haven for artists, writers, and their well-bred Brahmin backers. In 1811 its founders also created the *North American Review,* which is published to this day. One of the oldest cultural institutions and the largest membership library in North America, the Athenaeum moved to its current home here in 1849. By 1851, it was one of the five largest libraries in America, boasting 50,000 volumes—the same number as the Library of Congress. Feminist journalist Margaret Fuller studied here, as did transcendentalist philosopher Ralph Waldo Emerson. Statesman Daniel Webster whiled away the hours in Athenaeum stacks, as did essayists, authors, and poets like Oliver Wendell Holmes, Lydia Maria Child, Amy Lowell, and Henry Wadsworth Longfellow. Novelist Nathaniel Hawthorne once wrote about meeting a ghost in the Boston Athenaeum reading room. (Hawthorne often wandered the neighborhood here; a fan of graveyards and tombstone inscriptions, young Hawthorne may—or may not—have gotten inspiration for the Hester Prynne character of *The Scarlet Letter* from a headstone in the nearby King's Chapel Burying Ground.)

Down the street from Parker's stood the Old Corner Bookstore, which was a magnet for poets, authors, and philosophers, especially from the years 1845 to 1865, when entrepreneurs William D. Ticknor and James T. Fields revolutionized the world of American book publishing. Ticknor and Fields' Old Corner Bookstore was more than a well-stocked bookshop and a prominent publishing house. It was also a mecca for the literary world, where renowned authors would often be seen visiting and socializing with one another and basking in the light of "Jamie" Fields. To attract and endear authors to his firm, Fields devised the first known system of royalties and secured ownership of prestigious magazines like the *North American Review* and *The Atlantic Monthly,* in which his writers regularly appeared. He was also a friend, confidante, publicist, and tour promoter for his authors. Along with his wife, author Annie Adams Fields, Jamie held cozy, creative salons for writers, thinkers, and artists in the couple's Charles Street home. (The Houghton Mifflin Company, still based in Boston, is a direct descendant of Ticknor & Fields publishing house.)

Originating in the Literary Club and the Magazine Club, two private associations of the mid-1850s, the Saturday Club began as a small group of friends who chose the Parker House to host their festive roundtables on the last Saturday afternoon of every month. Typical among its nineteenth-century members was poet, essayist, and preeminent transcendentalist Ralph Waldo Emerson. Emerson would take the

The presence of the Old Corner Bookstore down the street ensured the Parker House a literary clientele.

Directly up the street from the Parker House was the Boston Athenaeum.

Thoreau and The Parker "Smoke House"

An astonishing number of mid-nineteenth century American *literati* and intellectuals called Greater Boston home. Many of these men—from Emerson, Lowell, Holmes, Hawthorne, Whittier, and Longfellow to Charles Francis Adams, Francis Parkman, Louis Agassiz, and John Sullivan Dwight—also attended the prestigious Saturday Club, which met at the Parker House the last Saturday of each month.

Though Henry David Thoreau was friend to many Saturday Club members and the author of one of the era's most enduring literary classics, *Walden, or, Life in The Woods* (1854), he was not fond of such elitist gatherings nor of the smoke-filled hotel where they were held.

> As for the Parker House, I went there once, when the club was away, but I found it hard to see through the cigar smoke, and men were deposited about in chairs over the marble floor, as thick as legs of bacon in a smoke house. It was all smoke…

This ambrotype portrait of Thoreau was taken by Daniel Ricketson at E.S. Dunshee's establishment in New Bedford, Massachusetts, August, 1861. Though he was 44 years old at the time, Thoreau looks much older, perhaps due to the tuberculosis which caused his death less than a year later.

> The only room in Boston I visit with alacrity is the Gentlemen's room at the Fitchburg Depot, where I wait for the cars [trains], sometimes for two hours, in order to get out of town. It is a paradise to the Parker House, for no smoking is allowed…and I am pretty sure to find someone there whose face is set the same way as my own.

It must be noted that the "gentleman's room" Thoreau references is not the bathroom but the waiting room. And, as one might guess, smoking is no longer allowed at the modern Omni Parker House!

As with most nineteenth-century clubs, hotels, bars, and restaurants, Saturday Club meetings at the Parker House were smoke-filled events.

train from his home in Concord, then visit the Old Corner Bookstore and the Athenaeum before dining at the Parker House. Alongside Emerson might be poet and *The Atlantic Monthly* editor James Russell Lowell, scientist Louis Agassiz, novelist Nathaniel Hawthorne, poets John Greenleaf Whittier and Henry Wadsworth Longfellow, diplomat Charles Francis Adams, historian Francis Parkman, sage-about-town Dr. Oliver Wendell Holmes, and many others.

The Saturday Club's afternoons were often taken up with poetry readings, impassioned discussions, and book critiques. Indeed, according to enduring urban legends, some great moments in literary history transpired in these Parker House meetings. Here, in the folds of the Saturday Club, Longfellow drafted portions of "Paul Revere's Ride," the idea for *The Atlantic Monthly* was born, and Dickens gave his first American reading of *A Christmas Carol* (All of these claims have been contested, but none definitively proven one way or the other). As important to the group as intellectual pursuit, however, was camaraderie—and a hefty dose of mirth, gossip, revelry, and seven-course meals, all washed down with endless elixirs.

Literary superstar Charles Dickens, who resided at the Parker House during his 1867-68 American lecture tour, joined club members for one particularly memorable meeting, on November 30, 1867. Among the author's noted contributions was a favorite gin punch—concocted on site, after Dickens dispatched his assistant George Dolby to pull a stash of fine gin off a Cunard liner docked nearby.

Dickens' presence in Boston always created a stir. When staying at the Parker House, he took lengthy walks almost every afternoon, dressed flamboyantly in a brightly colored coat and shiny boots, accessorized with striped cravat, fine hat, and gloves. Guards were regularly assigned to his hotel room door, since curious fans were

Emerson   Hawthorne   Longfellow

The literary gentlemen above were among the illustrious members of the Saturday Club. The screened diagram, drawn by John Sullivan Dwight, shows the seating arrangement at one club meeting.

Forever Dickens

English superstar author Charles Dickens has been a constant presence at the Parker House since staying here during his 1867-68 stateside lecture tour.

When he spoke at the nearby Tremont Theatre, Dickens used his classic stage props: gas lamps lighting a large maroon backdrop, a waist-high podium desk with a block for resting his elbow, and a rail below for his foot. Dickens began his two-hour performances precisely at eight o'clock, opening with a 90-minute reading, followed by a short intermission, then ending with a second, short reading.

Over the past century and a half, Dickens' works, his name, his spirit, his attire, his room décor, and his ghost have all become part of the fabric at the Omni Parker House.

A pensive Dickens is captured in this nineteenth century engraving by F.T. Stuart of Boston.

Above: In 1927, Parker House players invoke the spirit of Dickens in their costumed revelry.

Left: The Dickens Room at the Omni Parker House includes the mantel from Dicken's 1867-68 stay.

48

Descendants of Charles Dickens have periodically made appearances and done readings at the Omni Parker House.

Actor Mark Dickens, the novelist's great-great grandson, visits the hotel to perform a rendition of A Christmas Carol.

Actor Al LePage presents an evening of Dickens' readings to an attentive audience in the Press Room.

Dickens was a flamboyant dresser and exuberant performer when reading to his overflow audiences. He knew his material so intimately that the book was little more than a prop.

49

eager to catch a glimpse of their favorite writer rehearsing the exaggerated gestures and odd facial expressions he used to create characters in his public readings. The colorful Dickens preened and practiced his animated talks in front of a large mirror that now rests in the mezzanine-level hall by the Press Room. Artifacts from his stay were long kept on display in the Dickens Room. Today, that room is used for meeting and dining, but it still holds the marble fireplace mantle Dickens used.

Animation got the better of Dickens one festive night at the Saturday Club, incidentally. Annie Adams Fields, in *Memories of a Hostess* (1922), remembered the evening well:

> *After the dinner (at the Parker) the other night,*
> *Mr. Dickens thought he would take a warm bath; but,*
> *the water being drawn, he began playing the clown*
> *in pantomime on the edge of the bath (with his clothes on)…*
> *[I]n a moment, and before he knew where he was,*
> *he had tumbled in head over heels, clothes and all.*

Literary luminaries still gather at the Omni Parker House today. In March of 1999, for example, the new Literary Trail of Greater Boston (and its companion book, by the author of this volume) was launched in a gala dinner on School Street, inspiring a *Tab* newspaper reporter to wax eloquent on past and present:

Perhaps not since the days of the 19th-century regular meetings of the literary Saturday Club have so many literati darkened the doorstep of the Omni Parker House Hotel as did Thursday evening the week before last… The Boston History Collaborative hosted some of the more brilliant minds of Boston (nary a politician in sight…). [It was] one of the few times a person might bump into the economic expert of the 20th century John Kenneth Galbraith…and then turn around and chat with the author of "All I Need to Know I Learned From My Cat," Suzy Becker. Others engaged in cerebral small talk included Houghton Mifflin senior vice president Gary Smith; author James Carroll and wife, Alexandra Marshall; author David McCullough, who shared tales of his literary past over dinner; Brandeis University Prof. David Hackett Fischer…

Twain & Howells: Parker House Pals

In March of 1877, humorist Mark Twain was staying at the Parker House in room 168. A reporter from the *Globe* entered Twain's room, shuttled in by a porter. After a pause of several moments, Twain swiveled around in his large easy chair and faced his visitor.

With a local newspaper in hand and puffing on a large cigar, Twain observed to the reporter, "You see for yourself that I'm pretty near heaven—not theologically, of course, but by the hotel standard."

This cropped photographic portrait of Mark Twain was taken by Mathew Brady on February 7, 1871.

Samuel Clemens, a.k.a. Mark Twain, was a frequent visitor to The Hub. Sometimes he was here for book tours, sometimes for lectures—and almost always to connect with his friend William Dean Howells, who was editor of the prestigious *Atlantic Monthly* from 1871 to 1881.

Twain and Howells had met in 1869, when Howells served as the magazine's assistant editor, under famed publisher and Old Corner Bookstore owner, James. T. Fields. Assigned to find new literary voices from the West, Howells chose to review Twain's *The Innocents Abroad* in *The Atlantic's* December 1869 issue. He complimented the little-known Twain in his review, closing with, "It is no business of ours to fix his rank among the humorists California has given us, but we think he is, in an entirely different way from all the others, quite worthy of the company of the best."

While this issue was still on the newsstands, a six-foot, red-headed Twain marched into the *The Atlantic Monthly* office at 124 Tremont, just a five-minute walk from the Parker House. Unannounced and surely unexpected, Twain explained that he was looking for the author of the review. As it turned out, Twain proved amusing and grateful; Howells was struck by this talented writer, who barreled into the office wearing a sealskin coat "with the fur out;" and their friendship took off.

It's likely that Twain and Howells frequented the Parker House together over the years. Howells was, after all, a second-generation member of the Saturday Club, which held court at Parker's. Though many of Howell's literary colleagues were initially not terribly fond of Twain—calling his irreverent antics and attitude "buffoonery"—Howells proved a steadfast friend and supporter. Howells also began publishing installments of Twain stories in *The Atlantic* as early as 1875.

Twain's Boston friend and supporter, William Dean Howells, was photographed by George Kendall Warren circa 1875-1882.

When not in Boston, the two friends often chatted and dined at Howell's home across the Charles River, at 37 Concord Avenue, Cambridge. Both men profited from this friendship and professional literary relationship that ended up lasting almost half a century: during that time, Howells became the acknowledged "Dean of American Letters" and Twain became, well, Mark Twain.

Innocence and The Parker House

Edith Wharton

Author Edith Wharton was well aware of how the "the other half" lived. Born in 1862, she was christened Edith Newbold Jones—not any old Joneses, mind you, but the extraordinarily rich family that reportedly inspired the phrase "keeping up with the Joneses."

As a member of a wealthy, privileged, socially well-connected household, Edith spent her life in all the right places—like upper crust neighborhoods in New York City, Newport, Rhode Island, and Europe, as well as in her summer mansion, "The Mount," in bucolic Lenox, Massachusetts.

As a result of these experiences, when Wharton wrote about well-healed characters in her stories, poems, and novels, those characters stayed in all the right places as well. In the case of Countess Ellen Olenska and Newland Archer, the illicit lovers of *The Age of Innocence,* that translated into a simple rule: when in Boston, stay at the Parker House.

The *Age of Innocence,* published in 1920, was a novel about fashionable New York Society in the 1870s. The book garnered Wharton a Pulitzer Prize in 1921, making her the first woman awarded the Pulitzer Prize for fiction.

In Chapter XXIII of the book, Archer journeys to Boston in the hopes of bumping into his old paramour, Countess Olenska. After a futile trip to the Parker House, he finds her on a bench in the Common, and begins an awkward conversation.

"You're alone—at the Parker House?" he asks incredulously. She responds, flashing her old malice, saying "Does it strike you as dangerous?… unconventional? I see; I suppose it is."

The Parker House, of course, was used to catering to well-healed women traveling alone, and even boasted an elegant dining room especially for ladies. But poor, sad Archer was clueless about the New Century or the New Woman who moved through it with surprising aplomb.

"You're alone—at the Parker House?" he asks incredulously.

She responds, flashing her old malice, saying "Does it strike you

as dangerous?…unconventional? I see; I suppose it is."

Willa Cather's Parker House Home

Willa Cather is remembered as an esteemed American author whose novels of frontier life on the Great Plains include such classics as O Pioneers!, My Antonia, and The Song of the Lark. Though she was born in Virginia, raised in Nebraska, worked in Pittsburgh, and was based in New York for the majority of her life, it was Boston where she made many of the the connections that helped develop her literary career.

In 1906, Cather moved to Manhattan to join the staff of McClure's magazine. Her first major assignment was editing and co-writing a biography of Mary Baker Eddy, the Boston-based founder of the First Church of Christ, Scientist. In order to be nearer to Mrs. Eddy and the Christian Science Mother Church, Cather spent most of 1907 living at the Parker House on School Street. Mary Baker Eddy: The Story of Her Life and the History of Christian Science, co-written with Georgina Milmine, was published in McClure's in fourteen installments between 1907 and 1908, then later in book form.

The Parker House, as it turns out, was a perfect home-away-from-home for Cather. The ghosts of many of her literary heroes— Ralph Waldo Emerson, Nathaniel Hawthorne, Charles Dickens, and Henry James—were part of the fabric at the hotel, since it had been their regular Saturday Club haunt. Even better were the living authors she met and befriended during her Parker House stay.

While in Boston, Cather became close with Annie Adams Fields—the widow of Jamie Fields of Old Corner Bookstore fame—and her companion, author Sarah Orne Jewett. Cather joined the couple for their prestigious literary salons at 148 Charles Street. Jewett in particular became a comrade and mentor to Cather—so much so that Cather dedicated O Pioneers! (1913), the first novel in her Prairie Trilogy, to her.

The Boston connection continued long after her Parker House residencey as well, since Houghton Mifflin subsequently published many of Cather's later books.

Above: In this 1912 black and white photo by Aime Dupont, Willa Cather wears a necklace from Sarah Orne Jewett.

Left to right: Mary Baker Eddy, Sarah Orne Jewett, and Annie Adams Fields.

PARTY POLITICS

Boston's City Hall was built facing the Parker House School Street entrance in 1865—only a decade after the hotel's opening. Since the seat of Massachusetts government was just up the road, on the crest of Beacon Hill, the Parker House was directly on the "hot line" between City Hall and the State House—a fortuitous situation that ensured regular political clientele for more than a century. State and local politicians dined and drank at Parker's, hunkering down daily for pleasure, politicking, or clandestine tête-a-têtes. Moreover, the Parker House attracted pols of national stature as well: it is claimed that every U.S. Chief of State from Ulysses S. Grant through William J. Clinton passed through the hotel's portals, stayed in its suites, lobbied in its Press Room, imbibed in its bars, or dined in its restaurants.

The twentieth-century president most closely associated with Massachusetts, John Fitzgerald Kennedy, had an earlier start than most at the Parker House. Legendary

BOSTON'S GOLDEN MILE-MARKER

One of the reasons the Omni Parker House has remained a favorite haunt for politicians over the last century and half is its proximity to the Massachusetts State House. When driving to The Hub, you'll often see signs that tell you Boston is three, five, or some other number of miles away. Curiously, you are sometimes already *within* the Boston city limits when these signs appear. What's the story? The number of miles noted is specifically to the mile-marker center of Boston, the glittering golden dome of the State House. It's no wonder then that Dr. Oliver Wendell Holmes called our State House—and why folks still call Boston—"The Hub of the Solar System."

*The Parker House was situated directly on the "hot line"
between Boston's Old City Hall (left) and the
Massachusetts State House, on Beacon Hill (right).*

politician Clement Norton often recalled the day in 1923 when former Boston mayor John ("Honey Fitz") Fitzgerald was being celebrated with a Parker House party. "I saw this little boy sitting outside the hall, and I said to him, who are you waiting for, kid?" The boy, the six-year-old JFK, responded simply, "Grandpa." Norton reportedly took the youngster inside, then coached him to point at the former mayor and say, "This is the best grandfather a child ever had." (Other versions of the story have James Michael Curley lifting the boy on the table and urging him to speak.) Whatever the impetus, the crowd loved the boy's words, heralded as "Jack Kennedy's first public speech."

Twenty-three years later, Kennedy announced his candidacy for the U.S. Congress from the same site. By that time, he was a World War II hero whose valiant rescues on PT-109 were regularly recounted to the charmed voting public. Despite rumors to the contrary, Kennedy did not declare his candidacy for the U.S. Presidency at the Parker House in 1960. He did, however, propose marriage to Jacqueline Bouvier at Table 40 in Parker's Restaurant. JFK also held his subsequent bachelor party in the Press Room; that evening, JFK's friends presented him with an oil painting of the July 1953 cover of *Life* magazine, depicting Jack sailing near Hyannis with his fiancée.

The Kennedy Corner

The Parker House was, in many ways, a home away from home for John Fitzgerald Kennedy. Beginning in 1923, when little Jack made his "first public speech" here, Kennedy returned again and again to his favorite School Street destination for reasons and events that were both personal and political, and connected to fun, fundraising, family, campaigning, and public relations.

Though there are no known photos of Jack's proposal of marriage to Jacqueline Bouvier at Table 40 in Parker's Restaurant, images of both the table and the happy newlyweds are shown here. The other photos are a small sample of Kennedy's countless sojourns at the Parker House over a period of forty years.

The most colorful of all the Parker House's regular political patrons was surely James Michael Curley (1874-1958), the charismatic, Irish-American "Mayor of the Poor" who dominated Boston politics for the first half of the twentieth century. A mover, shaker, and spellbinding speaker, Curley became a cultural hero to underdogs in general—and to Boston's Irish in particular—while alternately serving as common councilor, alderman, state representative, congressman, Massachusetts governor, four-time Boston mayor, and two-time federal prison inmate. The roguish politician was also an inside dealer who frequently alienated old-time Yankee Brahmins and almost bankrupted the city of Boston with his welfare and city improvement programs.

Curley held court at daily luncheons in Parker's main dining room, delighting curious onlookers and impressing the waitstaff by tipping silver dollars. As a result of his endless politicking, valiant efforts, and dubious escapades, James Michael Curley became the stuff of legend: his life, thinly disguised in a character named Frank Skeffington, was retold in Edwin O'Connor's 1956 novel, *The Last Hurrah*. Spencer Tracy starred in the film version. Despite O'Connor's insistence that Skeffington was not modeled after the former mayor, it was rumored that Curley might sue the author for libel. As it became clear that *The Last Hurrah* was enhancing rather than tainting Curley's image, Curley began praising the book, and endorsing it as his own story. In a chance meeting with O'Connor outside the Parker House in 1956, Curley thanked O'Connor for the novel, adding that he particularly liked "the part where I die."

Curley did die two years later, in 1958. Needless to say, his legend lived on. In 1980, two life-like bronze statues of Curley—a folksy, seated version and a powerful, standing one—were created by sculptor Lloyd Lillie and installed near Faneuil Hall Marketplace, only a few blocks away from Old City Hall and the Parker House. In

Spencer Tracy played Frank Skeffington in the film version of The Last Hurrah.

According to reminiscences of late nineteenth century staff, one of the grandest events ever held at the Parker House was the 1875 party for President Ulysses S. Grant and his cabinet. "The President was taciturn and smoked black cigars all evening," remembered former bell-boy William J. O'Neil of Somerville, in a *Boston Globe* article dated November 22, 1925.

The Grant gala was sponsored by the Commercial Club and held in the old Crystal Room. After an introduction by club president, Alexander Hamilton Rice—a paper-product distribution magnate and prominent Republican politician—the crowd applauded enthusiastically and hurled napkins into the air. Not wanting to discuss public affairs in any way, nor willing to make a speech, Grant puffed again on his cigar, endured the accolades, and remained seated for the duration.

This half-length portrait of America's eminently successful Civil War general (and less successful eighteenth President) was taken between 1869 and 1885.

59

1992, author Jack Beatty reinvented Curley's oft-told tale in *The Rascal King*. In 1999, Boston University's prestigious Huntington Theatre Company hosted the world premiere of O'Connor's *The Last Hurrah*, adapted for the stage by Eric Simonson.

Since 1969, "The Last Hurrah" has also been the name of one of the Parker House's popular bars. The pub's original location was in the Parker House basement; it reopened in 1999 in its current street-level site, on the corner of School and Tremont. The newest incarnation of the Last Hurrah, incidentally, is a perfect place to meet friends and colleagues, to eat and drink (recent accolades include *Whiskey Magazine*'s "Great Whiskey Bar of the World" award), and to watch America walk by on Boston's historic Freedom Trail, which passes right outside.

In a "Saloon of the Week" column, *Boston Globe* veteran journalist Mike Barnicle observed, "The Last Hurrah is a saloon, a clubhouse, a meetinghouse. It is as much a part of Boston as the Freedom Trail." More than just an inviting, prize-winning pub

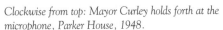

The Curley Decades

James Michael Curley—the charismatic, Irish-American "Mayor of the Poor" who dominated Boston politics for the first half of the twentieth century—was a constant presence at the Parker House. The popular Omni Parker House bar, *The Last Hurrah*, was named for Edwin O'Connor's 1956 novel of the same name, a thinly disguised chronicling of Curley's colorful life and the world in which he lived.

Clockwise from top: Mayor Curley holds forth at the microphone, Parker House, 1948.

Curley was a significant supporter of Franklin D. Roosevelt in FDR's presidential campaigning in the Bay State, 1932.

Representatives of the Veterans of Foreign Wars pin a citizen's service medal on Curley at the Parker House, 1948.

Governor-elect Curley addresses the mayors of the Commonwealth's cities and towns at the Parker House, 1934.

In a chance meeting with Edwin O'Connor outside the Parker House in 1956, Curley thanked the author for his novel, The Last Hurrah, *adding that he particularly liked "the part where I die." In this 1958 image from* The Boston Herald, *O'Connor passes by Curley's coffin, laying in state at the Massachusetts State House.*

THE
LAST HURRAH

by EDWIN O'CONNOR

An Atlantic Monthly Press Book
LITTLE, BROWN AND COMPANY · Boston, Toronto

Curley in front of old City Hall, with his beloved Parker House in the background, 1947.

Boston's new City Hall under construction.

in a great location, The Last Hurrah is also a mini-museum of twentieth-century Boston: framed photos of Curley and friends in their heyday, plus images of a host of celebrated individuals associated with Boston and the Parker House, line the walls.

Boston's City Hall moved to the newly constructed Government Center in 1969. Happily, the old City Hall building was spared demolition and reincarnated as office and restaurant space. Though the Omni Parker House is no longer on the path from City Hall to the State House, the hotel maintains its political appeal. Some of the more recent visits by high-profile politicians have been joyous events—like Bill Clinton's successful fundraiser of 1991, Rudy Giuliani's keynote speech here during the 2004 Democratic National Convention, and gubernatorial campaigns by Mitt Romney, Kerry Healey, and Deval Patrick. Others have signaled sadder times: Massachusetts governor and Democratic presidential candidate Michael Dukakis, for example, announced the end of his political career at the Parker House, and Senator Paul Tsongas dropped out of the presidential race here, both in the early 1990s.

An interesting footnote to presidential politics at Parker's involves America's two best-known Chiefs of State, who—though they never set foot in the Parker House—surely trod on the ground where it stands today. George Washington attended services at King's Chapel, directly across the street; but his visit came eighty years before the hotel was built. Though Abraham Lincoln lectured at Tremont Temple, just around the corner, his Boston sojourn predated Parker's construction by several years. However, his wife, Mary Todd Lincoln, did stay here during a visit to Boston in 1862.

Teddy Kennedy
at the Parker House

Left: Ted and Kara Kennedy at a 1982 fundraiser in the Parker House Ballroom.

Below: A young Senator Kennedy speaks at the lectern for the Dunfey Parker House, 1970s.

Bottom: Excerpt of letter from Senator Kennedy to Manager Paul Sacco of the Omni Parker House, 1992.

Again, let me express my gratitude for your willingness to be of such great assistance. The Parker House has a significant place in some of the happiest memories of my family. Any collection in the Kennedy Library would not be complete without a representation of the contribution made by the Parker House on many an important occasion -- especially victorious election nights!

With all good wishes.

Sincerely,

my thanks.

Edward M. Kennedy

THEATRICAL PURSUITS

Many nineteenth-century actors and opera stars were familiar with this neighborhood well before the Parker House was built. As previously noted, the popular Tremont Theatre (1828-1843) was located around the corner (after its reincarnation as a church, Tremont Temple continued to host theatrical productions). Meanwhile, several other significant stages of the nineteenth century —including the Boston Museum, the Boston Theatre, and the Howard Athenaeum—were situated close to the Parker House as well.

Because of its proximity, as well as its enduring appeal, Parker House guests included such world-class entertainers as Sarah Bernhardt, Adelina Patti, Ellen Terry, Edwin Booth, Richard Mansfield, Henry Irving, Augustin Daly, and Charlotte Cushman. Cushman (1816-1876) was the first of America's great ladies of the stage, remembered as much for her powerful presence as for her ability to play male and female roles with equal flair. Born in Boston's North End, Cushman was one of the numerous celebrities who actually lived in the Parker House; following eighteen years of "farewell performances," Cushman also died there.

One of the theater-world guests Harvey Parker rarely discussed was actor Edwin Booth's brother, John Wilkes Booth. Edwin Booth (1833-1893) was a world-class tragedian who made his theatrical debut at the Boston Museum on Tremont Street in 1849. Eight years later, at the age of twenty-three, Edwin headlined at the Boston Theatre on Washington Street as Sir Giles Overreach. That victorious performance proved the turning point of his career and officially began his thirty-year reign as *the* American actor of note. Meanwhile, as Edwin was conquering audiences in the Northeast, another brother, Junius, Jr., was impressing the Midwest with his acting skills.

Younger brother John Wilkes, ten years Edwin's junior, was arguably the least talented actor in this theatrical family. While Edwin came to specialize in difficult dramatic roles like Hamlet and Richelieu, John tended towards fluffier stuff, enamoring female fans with his dashing swordplay, daring leaps, flashing eyes, and impassioned gestures. He was a charming matinee idol, an unabashed ladies' man—

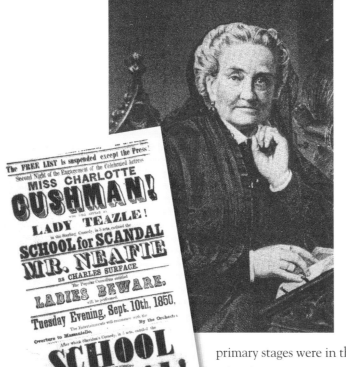

Actress Charlotte Cushman, the first of America's great leading ladies, made the Parker House her permanent residence.

and an ardent Confederate sympathizer. Though his primary stages were in the South, John Wilkes played elsewhere as well. In 1864, for example, all three Booth brothers collaborated in a New York production of *Julius Caesar*, and John played the romantic hero of *The Marble Heart* at the Boston Museum.

During the 1860s, the Booths' stage careers grew as the Civil War ravaged America. Edwin believed in the Union cause and proudly cast his first vote ever for Abraham Lincoln in the mid-war elections of 1863. Southern-based John Wilkes fervently disagreed. "When I told him I had voted for Lincoln's re-election, he expressed deep regret, and declared his belief that Lincoln would be made king of America," wrote Edwin in an 1881 letter. "This, I believe, drove him beyond the limits of reason."

On April 5 and 6, 1865, John Wilkes was registered at the Parker House and was seen eating in its restaurant. It's possible that he went to visit brother Edwin, who was playing a successful three-week engagement at the 3,000-seat Boston Theatre. It was reported in the *Boston Evening Transcript* of April 15 that he was indeed practicing his aim: "[A man named] Borland…saw Booth at Edwards' shooting gallery [near Parker's], where Booth practiced pistol firing in various difficult ways such as between his legs, over his shoulder and under his arms."

Eight days after leaving Boston, on April 14, 1865, John Wilkes Booth assassinated President Lincoln at Ford's Theatre in Washington, D.C.

Lincoln as photographed by Alexander Hesler, Springfield, Illinois, June 3, 1860

Boston, March 19, 1859.

Dear Sir:—

You are respectfully invited to attend a Festival, at the Parker House, in this city, on Wednesday, April 13th (next,) at 3 P. M., in honor of the birth-day of THOMAS JEFFERSON, *the father of the "ordinance of 1787," and the apostle of State Rights.*

Please favor the Committee with an early reply.

Your obedient servants, Henry L Pierce

Wm J Robinson

W Silloton   *Committee.*

Albert G Browne,

F. W. Bird.

1672

The Lincolns' Log

Though Abraham Lincoln's second (and last) visit to Boston was in the spring of 1859—a year before he assumed the Presidency—he failed to make a stop at the Parker House. We know that he was invited to visit the hotel, however, since an invitation, dated March 19, 1859, still exists.

Dear Sir:
You are respectfully invited to attend a Festival, at the Parker House, in this city, on Wednesday, April 13th (next,) at 3 P.M., in honor of the birthday of THOMAS JEFFERSON, the father of the "ordinance of 1787," and the apostle of State Rights. Please favor the Committee with an early reply. Your obedient servants.......

Lincoln's response, dated April 6, 1859, was mailed from Springfield, Illinois, and addressed to the invitation's signers, "Messrs. Henry L. Pierce, & others." It began with polite regrets:

Gentlemen—Your kind note inviting me to attend a Festival in Boston, on the 13th. Inst. in honor of the birth-day of Thomas Jefferson, was duly received. My engagements are such that I can not attend.

Though the missive could have stopped there, Lincoln went on to pen a hefty 600-word thought piece, suggesting perhaps that his intention was to have his letter read aloud at the Parker House festival. After referencing the history of American political parties, an allusion to Euclid, and familiar arguments from his most recent speeches, Lincoln ended with an eminently quotable anti-slavery passage that aptly referenced Jefferson and liberty:

This is a world of compensations; and he who would be no slave, must consent to have no slave. Those who deny freedom to others, deserve it not for themselves; and, under a just God, can not long retain it.

All honor to Jefferson—to the man who, in the concrete pressure of a struggle for national independence by a single people, had the coolness, forecast, and capacity to introduce into a merely revolutionary document, an abstract truth, applicable to all men and all times, and so to embalm it there, that to-day, and in all coming days, it shall be a rebuke and a stumbling-block to the very harbingers of re-appearing tyranny and oppression.

Your obedient Servant — A.Lincoln

When Lincoln ran for the Presidency the following year, he carried liberal Massachusetts with ease. Moreover, many of Boston's most radical abolitionists—like William Lloyd Garrison, Julia Ward Howe, and Wendell Phillips—maintained pressure on the new President to keep his anti-slavery ideals amidst the intense stresses and compromises of the Civil War.

The Presidents' wife, Mary Todd Lincoln, was an unusually well-traveled woman for her time. Seeking relaxation from what she perceived as "the arduous cares and duties of the White House," the First Lady often went on excursions during Lincoln's presidency. While traveling, she indulged in her problematic pastime: Power Shopping.

During some of the darkest days of the war, Mrs. Lincoln came to Boston as part of a five-week sojourn away from the nation's capital and stayed at the Parker House. In addition to shopping, one of her missions was to see her son, Robert Todd, who was attending Harvard College.

Robert Todd Lincoln had begun undergraduate studies at Harvard in 1860, eventually graduating with the Class of 1864. Since the student body was primarily Republican at the time, a *New York Times* reporter observed that Robert had "grown vastly in popularity with his fellow students and the townspeople generally" after his father's election to the Presidency. It's likely that young Robert frequented, or at least visited, the Parker House while at Harvard, since his schoolmates were notorious imbibers there. Humorist Artemus Ward, one of President Lincoln's favorite writers, noted that during the Civil War, "[Harvard College], this celebrated institootion of learnin' is pleasantly situated in the Bar-room of Parker's, in Scool street…"

On November 9, 1862, President Lincoln addressed a telegram to his wife at the Parker House. Though Mrs. Lincoln was expert at eluding newspaperman, the word got out about her presence in town. On November 10, a cheering crowd gathered in the streets outside the Parker House while a band serenaded the First Lady. According to newspaper reports, she graciously waved her handkerchief to the gathering below and appeared several times at her hotel window.

Articles and letters in the *Boston Post* of November 11 and the *Boston Courier* of November 12 told of—and sometimes complained about—Mrs. Lincoln's trip. Her party had apparently claimed an entire railroad car for themselves en route to Boston, inconveniencing several dozen other passengers. She also arrived in the city at 1:00 a.m., four hours later than scheduled and in the middle of a snowstorm.

67

This Mary Todd Lincoln carte de visite is an engraving based on a photo taken by Mathew B. Brady in Washington, D.C., 1861. The inaugural gown depicted is presumably Mrs. Lincoln's first. The baby pearl necklace is a piece from Tiffany's.

Robert Todd Lincoln, son of President Abraham and Mary Todd Lincoln, is shown in a seated, half-length portrait, circa 1865.

The worlds of drama and literature have happily collided at the Parker House over the decades—most notably in the person of Charles Dickens. As mentioned earlier, the popular British author made the Parker House home base during his 1867-68 American lecture tour and was known for performing his readings with theatrical flair. In 1999, actor Gerald Charles Dickens, the novelist's great-great grandson, reminisced at the Omni Parker House while appearing in a critically acclaimed one-man rendition of *A Christmas Carol* at Tremont Temple. Tremont Temple was the same stage where great-great granddad played his classic tale to an audience that included Henry Wadsworth Longfellow and Oliver Wendell Holmes, Sr.

History repeated itself in the special menu the Omni Parker House offered guests during Dickens' 1999 stay: oysters with caviar, roast filet of beef forestière, and duchess potatoes—the same victuals served to the late, great author in 1867!

The city of Boston declared Saturday, October 8, 2005, "Omni Parker House 150th Anniversary Day." On November 29, 2005, as part of ongoing Omni Parker House 150th Anniversary Gala Celebrations, several hundred VIP clients and select press enjoyed a festive reception in the Rooftop Ballroom and listened to Mark Dickens—yet another great-great grandson of Charles Dickens—give a special reading of *A Christmas Carol*. With an exclusive menu, samplings of past and present New England fare, a specialty bar featuring the Boston Cream Pie martini, and a demonstration of how to make Boston Cream Pie, the gala was the talk of the town.

PARKER HOUSE CURRENCY

At the outbreak of America's Civil War, an extraordinary demand for supplies produced abnormal trade conditions in Boston. Since small change had become scarce, many of the city's well-known business houses issued private scrip for about nine months, much of it printed by Louis Prang and Thomas Groom & Company. The Parker House was among the businesses that issued their own emergency currency in 1862. At the Parker House, scrip was printed in denominations of five, ten, twenty-five, and fifty cents, and used to make change or pay bills of less than one dollar. Some of the hotel scrip bore Harvey Parker's image, and all the currency was personally signed by him. A national banking law passed early in 1863 remedied the situation and ended the brief scrip era.

Bouncing Sarah Bernhardt

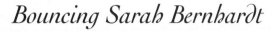

From the day Harvey Parker first opened his doors, theater people and their entourages were regular clientele and a welcome presence at the Parker House. Among those warmly welcomed thespians was France's leading actress, the internationally-acclaimed Sarah Bernhardt. The original Drama Queen, who was known as much for her eccentric habits as her prodigious acting talent, is perhaps best remembered for snoozing in a coffin that she kept with her much of the time.

During one of her many, *many* "farewell tours" that stretched from 1880 to 1918, however, the Divine Sarah was denied her request for a suite at the Parker House. It was not because of the coffin. Nor was it the large coterie of friends, admirers, and servants that hovered constantly about her, both at home and abroad. Instead, the problem was Bernhardt's penchant for traveling with a small army of beloved pets—and insisting they stay with her in her suite. As a writer for the old *Boston Post* observed, "When Mme. Bernhardt came to Boston … she brought with her a small menagerie. There was 'Toto,' the pet snake, a big fellow four or five feet long; 'Mechant,' the French 'possum, in a cage, and a big dog of uncertain breed, called 'Poulicide'." It could have been worse—since Bernhardt had made other tours accompanied by a cheetah, a lion cub, an alligator and seven chameleons, as well as the stuffed bat which she wore on her head.

But the Parker House responded with a politely emphatic "No."

Not to be outdone, Mme Bernhardt, according to the *Post* reporter, "glided … in all her majestic dignity out of the lobby…"

"When Mme. Bernhardt came to Boston … she brought with her a small menagerie. There was 'Toto,' the pet snake, a big fellow four or five feet long; 'Mechant,' the French 'possum, in a cage, and a big dog of uncertain breed, called 'Poulicide'."

"I love the character of the building and I love the people.

Otherwise I wouldn't have stayed here!"

*Bell-person Eddie Cotto in the lobby
of the Omni Parker House*

The Friends Of Eddie Cotto

It's the spring of 2013, and Edward John Cotto is sitting in the main lobby of the Omni Parker House, preparing for an interview. Handsomely outfitted in a dark business suit, pressed white shirt, and pin-striped tie, he's probably not immediately recognizable to his many friends and fans. Most of them are used to seeing Eddie in a bell-person's uniform, graciously transporting guests' suitcases and sundries in and out of the hotel.

Being a bell-person at the Omni Parker House is not just a job that Eddie loves. It's pretty much the only one he's ever had. Eddie knows the place inside and out—and has stories to tell that no one else even remembers. The reason: Eddie has had this gig for close to half a century.

Growing up in the Mission Hill neighborhood of Boston, Eddie had connections to Boston's most historic hotel even as a child. Longtime Parker House bellman, John Brehm, actually lived in Eddie's uncle's Mission Hill house for some six decades. But it wasn't until Eddie was around fifteen years old, and wandering down Tremont Street one lazy afternoon, that he bumped into Brehm on site. Brehm invited Eddie inside the Parker House, and ended up asking if the teenager would be willing to help out with errands.

"The Bell Captain was like the boss of the lobby," explains Eddie today. "The Bell Captain wouldn't have to check with the manager to do something like this. Besides, I was underage!" Brehm paid Eddie $45 a week for his erranding, which was handed to him as cash in an envelope. He also earned extra tips from other staff members for tasks like making ticket runs to the theater district.

Initially, Eddie wasn't so sure his Parker House job was something that would last. "I told John…I don't think I'm cut out for this kind of work!" he muses now. But when Eddie turned eighteen—the legal age for such employment—he was told by John Brehm that bellman Eddie Forrester had just passed away. "John told me the position was open if I wanted it."

So Eddie Cotto became an official Parker House bellman—a position now referred to as bell-person. "The staff was mostly Irish and the waiters mostly black. And while 'porters' checked people out, 'bellmen' checked them in. There really was a bell at the front desk—one of those dome types that you hit on the top. And in the old days, they'd hit the bell and you were expected to jump. That's where they got the term 'bell hop'."

Eddie recalls that his initiation rites happened in the mid-1960s, when the Parker House was quite run down. Though longtime owner Glenwood Sherrard had died in 1958, it was still the Sherrard era at the hotel (*see story on page 92*). Glen's wife Jessie and son Andrew were running the hotel. "Andrew was a very nice man, but not a very good businessman," says Eddie. "He was very generous—and would give jobs to needy people even if he didn't have a position open. But it seemed to me he spent his money foolishly. Andrew once had a fight

with Edison [the local electric company] and got so mad at them that he went out and bought a generator and put it in the Parker House basement. It was a huge amount of money. But what the place really needed was color TVs, chairs…more practical and basic things."

When the Dunfey family took over the financially ailing Parker House in 1968, they renovated the facility, and eventually returned it to profitability. "The Dunfeys were a caring people," Eddie recalls. "They wanted the hotel to get back on its feet and start showing a profit."

In Eddie's view, the Dunfeys learned through trial and error—and were fortunate to be there as other major Boston events of the mid-1970s helped buoy the local economy. The Bicentennial activities of 1975-76, the Tall Ships coming to the Hub, the successful conversion of the ailing and antiquated Quincy Market area into a major tourist destination, and the pro-active work of Mayor Kevin White all helped revive Boston's old hotels—including the Dunfey's Parker House, which benefited from its prime location on the Freedom Trail

The result in Eddie's eyes? "They put the place on the map again!"

Bell Captain John Brehm stands outside the School Street entrance of the Parker House, circa 1992.

The bell staff of the Parker House in 1979 included young Eddie Cotto, fourth from right, and John Brehm, second from right.

The veteran Bell Staff at the Parker House [left to right] Aaron Withers, Jack Goddard, John Hurley, John Hamrock, Tom Wasiolek, Eddie Cotto, Earl Norton, John Brehm, and Dan McKenna, Jr. Not pictured: Ralph Kelley, Stanley Wasiolek, Dan McKenna, Sr., John Scaparotti, John Ryan, John Ryan, Jr., Frank McGuire and Jim McGuire.

Over the decades, Eddie Cotto has amassed myriad stories, some that can be printed, and some not. Among his favorite printable memories:

"One night I was on the 3:00-11:00 p.m. shift, and around 8:30 these guys came in and wheeled a big casket into the lobby—and left it there. I said, 'What's this? It can't just stay in the lobby, scaring all the people!' And the guy said to me, 'But it's part of the show, and we can't fit it in his room or in the elevators.'"

Eddie found a place the crew could store the burial casket, never looking inside it himself. *"I didn't want to find out!"* But he did appreciate that magician David Copperfield was staying at the Omni Parker House, and thought his girlfriend, supermodel Claudia Schiffer, *"was very polite and very pretty."*

"Anthony Athenas—of Anthony's Pier Four and a lot of other restaurants—used to actually live here. Even after World War II, a lot of people still lived in hotels. Athenas always loved the Parker House. He enjoyed fine dining. And he always gave me gift certificates as thanks!"

"Cassius Clay came here—before he was calling himself Muhammad Ali—for one of those muscular dystrophy telethons. I remember coming into the lobby and seeing all these photographers waiting for him. But he just pushed the reporters aside and ran over to the kids in wheelchairs. Then he did his 'I am the greatest' and the kids loved it! He spent way more time with the kids than with the press."

72

Hugh Hefner

Six to seven big Cadillac limos pulled up to the Parker House one day. *"Then the doors opened and out hopped all these bunnies,"* remembers Eddie. *"It was Hugh Hefner, who was in town because his daughter was graduating from Brandeis. He was dating Barbie Benton at the time—she was lovely. And he introduced himself to me and later gave me a $300 tip. Afterwards, all these bunnies were in his suite, just sitting around the living room. I was in awe!"*

Heavyweight champion Cassius Clay, later known as Muhammad Ali

Judy Garland

Then there was the female star of stage and screen that young Eddie didn't recognize at first. "When she wanted to get out of the car, she always waited for me to open the door so she could tip me. She never used the revolving doors, and always used the side doors, so we could open them and she could tip us again." The gracious tipper was Judy Garland, and the era was different than today. "People back then were more service-oriented. They dressed up more, were very polite, and liked being helped."

"Downstairs, where the gym and offices are now found, was the Grille Room, which specialized in fish—like tripe, salmon… It had a nautical motif, with a big ship wheel at the entrance and nets hanging from the ceiling. [In 1969] it became The Last Hurrah—they wanted a fresh, new look. Roy and Ruth Dunfey loved Annette and Ed Winiker of the Winiker Band, who performed there. All four of them lived in the Parker House." (see story on page 74)

"Where the General Manager's office is now was a barber shop. Al Moscardelli was the barber, and he rented space there forever. There was also a boot black down there." [Author's Note: Elio A. "Al" Moscardelli of Quincy owned the barbershop at the Parker House Hotel for 37 years before his retirement in 1987. His clientele included Supreme Court Justice Arthur Goldberg, Speaker of the House Thomas "Tip" O'Neill, Boston Pops Conductor Arthur Fiedler, slugger Babe Ruth, boxing champ Jack Dempsey, and most of Boston's mayors and the Bay State's governors.]

Maestro Arthur Fiedler and pianist David Crohan

"Tip" O'Neill

A vintage shot of Ed Winiker with sons, Bo and Bill

All That Jazz:
The Winiker Bands at The Last Hurrah

It's been argued that the Big Band Revival of the late 1970s began at the Parker House — more specifically, at the hotel's popular pub known as The Last Hurrah. Longtime fans of the musical Winiker family, who were The Last Hurrah's "house band" from 1977 through 1991, would surely agree with that theory.

But the story requires a little back peddling to understand fully.

As brothers Bo and Bill Winiker explain it, their father Ed always played music. Among their dad's early gigs was as a member of his college swing band at the University of Alabama, which he followed with service in the Second World War. When sons Bo and Bill were growing up in Millis, Massachusetts, they remember their dad as a gentleman farmer by day and a professional musician by night. After Hurricane Carol blew the farm away in 1954, however, music began to dominate Ed and his family's lives. Ten-year old Bo, 12-year old Bill, and Ed's wife Annette were all eventually drafted into what became known as The Winiker Family Band.

Bo Winiker shares his trumpet with members of the Last Hurrah wait staff, circa 1981.

The Bo Winiker Orchestra at the Last Hurrah, circa 1981.

"I played piano as a child," notes Annette, "but I never imagined I'd be in the band. When I woke up on Mother's Day one year, Eddie said he had a special gift for me. I walked into the room and there was this bass fiddle stretched out—and it was for me! So he helped me learn how to play and got me a teacher from the New England Conservatory. We began playing together right away, first in the living room, but then he began bringing us out on jobs. And yes, the story is true that what I really wanted for a Mother's Day present was a washer and a dryer. But the bass fiddle changed my whole life! In those days it was much more common for women to stay at home."

In the mid '70s, at the height of the disco era, the Winiker Family Band was regularly performing on the round-trip excursion boat between Boston and Provincetown. Their repertoire was eclectic, and any jazz they played was of the modern variety. But during long family chats in the P'town layover, father Ed had an epiphany: "It's time to bring back swing!" This was a challenge, since the Big Bands that specialized in swing died out after World War II, partly because of changing musical tastes and partly due to the huge expense of operating bands with sixteen players.

But Ed Winiker had an epiphany "and" a plan. He would revive the classic Big Band repertoire, but rewrite the old charts so the tunes could be played by a small (read: affordable) ensemble. With that economy of size in mind, Ed re-imagined the likes of Benny Goodman, Count Basie, Glenn Miller, and others for a six-piece band—the Winiker family plus a couple of other music professionals. The plan worked, and the results were astonishing. "It was an auditory illusion!" says Bill of the big sound their small combo was able to create.

Cut to 1977. Through a weekly Thursday evening gig at the Pub'n'Grub, the Winikers attracted employees of the Parker House, then run by the Dunfey family. The original contract was to play at The Parker House for one month. Once the word got out that a great swing dance band was in residency at the Last Hurrah, however, the crowds swelled— and the job ended up lasting six nights a week (plus Sunday afternoon jazz brunch) for fourteen years. Bostonians, college students, and tourists all packed the dance floor night after night, year after year. Bill glows when he remembers, "The crowd was a microcosm of diverse people. It was a true melting pot downstairs." "The band, the music, was such

Annual Senior Citizens New Year's Eve Day Dinner Dance with Mayor Raymond Flynn, Ed Winiker, Bo Winiker, and Bill Winiker.

Parker House General Manager Philip Georgas discussing the New Year's Eve plan with band manager, Annette Winiker.

A great tradition at the Parker House was the Sunday afternoon Swing Brunch with the Winiker Band. In the photo, Chef Joe Ribas and his staff prepare for brunch.

Dave Stuart spent the night listening to the Winiker Band at the Last Hurrah; the Eurythmics star is shown in photo with Bill Winiker and Harry Appleman.

a great draw," adds Bo. "It was American classical music."

Meanwhile, parents Ed and Annette were in residency in yet another way. Since driving back and forth to Millis every night became old very quickly, the Parker House offered them their own hotel room, where they lived for ten years. "We started on the second floor in the smallest room in the hotel," says Annette. "But the band was such a success, and made the Parker House so much money, that we kept graduating, and ended up in a suite on the tenth floor!"

The Winikers performed primarily in The Last Hurrah, but various incarnations of the group also played Sunday brunch in Parker's

Restaurant, as well as special events in Parker's Bar, the Press Room, the Rooftop Ballroom, and the Martin Luther King Room. The family even had to divide into three separate groups—the Ed, Bo, and Bill Winiker Bands—to keep up with the Parker House work as well as all the other gigs that grew through and during this period of great exposure.

Over the years, the stars literally came out for the Winikers. Big names like Bette Midler, Bonnie Raitt, Pat Metheny, or Dave Stewart and Annie Lenox of Eurythmics would wander back to their rooms at the Parker House after their outdoor "Concerts on the Common" or from nearby shows, then chat, drink, and sometimes sit in with the band. "Everyone knew Bette Midler was in the audience," the

Bill and Bo Winiker visit the Last Hurrah, the newest incarnation of their old stomping grounds.

brothers recall, "but she declined to sing a song. We all really hit it off. Bill was leading the band that night, and Bette got frisky, yanking him by the tie across a table. After the show, she stepped up on stage and performed 'Boogie Woogie Bugle Boy' and a couple of other songs with the band. The place went ballistic! And Bill phoned Norma Nathan, who ended up writing a major story about it in the *Boston Herald* the next day."

All good things come to an end, and when management changed at the Parker House in the late 1980s, so too did the never-ending Winiker gig. It began as a schedule cut-back, then little by little, disk jockeys eventually replaced the compact swing band.

The news was devastating at first. But ultimately, the family had no regrets. Bo and Bill agree: "The Dunfey family and the Parker House gave us high visibility and a forum for our band and music. We had so much fun for so many years, and really became part of the Dunfey family. As it turns out, our best years were still to come. But this hotel sped up the process of us getting known…and put us on the map. Plus, it all helped bring swing music back into the limelight in New England!"

Omni Parker House general manager John Murtha greets Bill and Bo Winiker in the hotel lobby, 2013.

ARCHITECTURALLY
SPEAKING

The "House that Harvey Built" was designed and developed in stages, both during Parker's lifetime and long thereafter. The original five-story structure—often referred to as the "marble palace"— was designed by William Washburn (1808-1890), who was both a Boston architect and city councilor. A New Hampshire native who resided in Massachusetts for many years, Washburn began as a builder, then evolved into a planner and superintendent. His greatest successes were in hotels, partly in New York (the Fifth Avenue and the Victoria) but primarily in Boston.

Washburn designed many of Boston' best-known hostelries of the mid-nineteenth century, including the Revere House, the Tremont House, the American House (rebuilt 1851), Young's Hotel, and the Adams House. Other notable buildings in his portfolio for the downtown neighborhood near the Parker House included the National Theatre, the second incarnation of Tremont Temple, as a well as a renovation of the Old State House in 1830 (with Isaiah Rogers) and a remodeling of the interior of the "new" State House in 1853.

Washburn presumably oversaw the architectural changes at the Parker House in the decade following its 1855 debut, adding a six-story wing in 1860 and raising the main building two more stories, in 1866. The new stories were tucked under a stylish mansard roof, crowned by ornate iron grillwork and a flagpole.

After Parker's death in 1884, his one-time partners and successors, Edward O. Punchard and Joseph H. Beckman, retained architect Gridley James Fox Bryant (1816-1899) to complete Parker's dream: adding yet another extension to the main building, this time in the form of an elaborate, narrow, eight-story structure on the corner of Tremont and School streets—land which Harvey had acquired in 1883.

Bryant, the son of noted railway pioneer Gridley Bryant, studied in his father's engineering office and that of Alexander Parris, a prominent architect-engineer whose most memorable work was Quincy Market. After opening his own architectural office at the corner of Court and Washington streets, Bryant-the-Younger began a prestigious six-decade career that ranged from designing custom houses and government buildings to churches, schoolhouses, and private residences across the nation.

A leading proponent of the "Boston Granite Style," Bryant frequently teamed up with other leading architects, including Arthur Gilman. Their projects together were the stuff Boston history is made of: the grid-iron street pattern of Boston's Back Bay, the Arlington Street Church, and Old City Hall—the latter, directly across from the Parker House on School Street. Other of Bryant's designs were Ballou Hall (the original building at Tufts College), Hathorn Hall (Bates College's original building), the second addition to the Massachusetts State House, the Charlestown State Prison and Charles Street Jail, Horticultural Hall on Tremont Street, Boston's Mercantile Wharf Building, and the Hub's State Street Block.

G.J.F Bryant's work on the 1886 Parker House was a spectacle to behold. The eight-story structure he added was compared to a French chateau of four hundred years earlier, a style (or at least a "notion") fashionable in the homes of millionaires. The new Parker House sported a marble sheath on its exterior, a pavilion roof, paneled

The original "marble palace" designed by architect William Washburn opened to the public in October, 1855. Note Horticultural Hall, partly hidden by a tree, to the immediate left of the Parker House.

By 1866, Harvey Parker had purchased and demolished Horticultural Hall, then added a wing to his original hotel on the corner of School Street and Chapman Place.

At the turn of the 20th century, electrified trolleys and horse-drawn carriages both passed by the Bryant-designed Parker House.

The "French Chateau" Parker House, designed by G.J.F Bryant in 1886, feature the distinctive bay windows that garnished the edge of the Tremont-School corner.

chimneys, peaked dormers, plus an iron balustrade overlooking the neighborhood. The building's new corner, on School and Tremont, featured a distinctive tier of rounded bay windows extending up to the sixth floor.

As it turned out, the Parker House was Bryant's last major commission.

The Parker House closed its doors on November 23, 1925 (though one 80-room wing remained open to guests), and was turned over to the wrecking crew that December. In the place of the old French chateau, Claude M. Hart, general manager of the J.R. Whipple Corporation, ordered a "new" Parker House built—preferably much more sedate and modern than the structure it was replacing.

The man selected to design the contemporary Parker House was G. Henri Desmond of Desmond & Lord Architects. Born in Watertown on February 22, 1876, the son of Irish immigrants, Desmond was educated in the public schools, followed by architectural studies in what historic sources vaguely describe as "the office of a well-known firm." In 1920, he and his wife, Vesti Hollis, and their young son were living in Brighton, in a house Desmond had designed.

Though Desmond had worked independently prior to this time—and was best known for his expansion and modernization of Charles Bulfinch's 1829 Maine State Capitol—he took on the Parker House commission with his business partner, the younger Israel Pierre Lord (1881-1973). The team's office was located just up the road from the Parker House, at 15 Beacon Street.

Desmond's 1927 Parker House was fourteen stories high, with polished black Quincy granite on the lower exterior facades, and limestone and buff colored brick above. The very practical and fire-proofed structure had all the comforts of old, and then some: lush, ornamented public chambers with oak paneling, artfully plastered ceilings, crystal chandeliers, bronze-detailed doors, and eight hundred guest rooms.

After their Parker House success, Desmond & Lord designed a variety of school buildings in the Greater Boston area as well as downtown Boston structures like the Boston Consolidated Gas Company Building and the Suffolk County Courthouse addition in Pemberton Square. They also created a number of bridges, including the Cottage Farm Bridge, the Dorchester Bay Bridge on Morrissey Boulevard, the Boston University Bridge in Cambridgeport, the Calvin Coolidge Bridge in Hadley, and Memorial Bridge in Attleboro.

After the original partners retired, the firm Desmond & Lord continued, undertaking large works in Boston through the end of the 1970s. Among their major projects were the

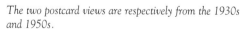

The two postcard views are respectively from the 1930s and 1950s.

Air Traffic Control Tower and the South Terminal Building at Logan Airport, the Mental Health Building at Boston University Medical Center, the Dock Square Parking Garage, Government Center, and the design, master planning, and construction of the University of Massachusetts Dartmouth Campus—the latter in collaboration with Paul Rudolph.

When the Parker House reopened on May 12, 1927, general manager Hart had his secretary, Miss Alice Mulligan, demonstrate the end of the old and beginning of the new. Miss Mulligan was flown over Boston Harbor by pilot Ralph T. Wickford, who guided the plane as Mulligan ceremoniously dumped the keys to the old Parker House into the water, from a height of some one thousand feet.

Was it all too newfangled for the very traditional Boston? Apparently not. For on May 15, the *Boston Globe* reassured its readers that, "Despite the fact that the new hotel is modern in every way, the traditions, spirit, and general atmosphere of the old Parker House, beloved by countless Bostonians and visitors from other cities, have been retained."

The 21st-century Omni Parker House

The Late Victorian Parker House

At the turn of the twentieth century, the interior of the Parker House was lavished with what modern critics might call "Victorian excess." In an outright denial of stylistic simplicity, growing numbers of wealthy travelers and locals wanted to frequent hotels, restaurants, and clubs where the unwritten rule was "Too Much is Not Enough." The decorative arts in this late Victorian Era—as evidenced in these indoor images of the Parker House—were filled with frills, grand ornamentation, overstuffed chairs, and an ornate and eclectic revival of historic styles.

In a turn-of-the century article about the Parker House, the writer praised the magnificence of the hotel after its most recent renovation:

"This is unquestionably the finest piece of hotel architecture in Boston...the popular resort of the wealthy, refined, and cultured circles of the public. ...The lofty, light basement is utilized for an elegant bar, café, and lunch-room. On the first floor are office, reading room, news stand, telegraph-office, café, and bar; also the ladies and gentlemen's dining-rooms, spacious and beautifully fitted up and decorated. On the second floor are the parlors—magnificent apartments, luxuriously furnished... Adjoining are the magnificent banquet-halls, which are SO deservedly popular and so justly famous, where in the course of a twelvemonth all the learned and prominent of the social, political, and commercial world gather to discuss, over the bountiful boards of the Parker House, the live topics of the day."

This building was demolished in 1925, and replaced by the Parker House we know today, which held its grand opening in 1927.

1. Ferns were a popular Victorian motif that worked well in cool, dark chambers, such as the main dining room at the Parker House; 2. Parker House offices; 3. The library featured overstuffed chairs, wall-to-wall books, and elegant classical columns; 4. A typical Parker House parlor.

The "Modern" 1927 Parker House

The "new" Parker House building that opened on May 12, 1927, had essentially the same exterior shell we see today. The interior, however, was another matter altogether, as evidenced in these images.

1. The lobby, as seen from the Tremont Street entrance in 1927.

2. Today's Parker's Bar was a library with "over three thousand interesting books on its shelves."

3. The appeal of Parker's "modern" bedrooms included ample double beds, full bathrooms with both tub and shower bath, bowls with hot and cold water, and mattresses and pillows "just like at home." Room prices ranged from $3.50-$7.00 per day, with suites costing a tad more.

4. The slightly pricier suites included parlors like the one shown here.

5. The Boston Bar Association maintained its own suite at the Parker House; the lounge, here, was a favorite hangout for members.

6. Food for all the Parker eateries was cooked and prepared in clean modern kitchen spaces.

7. The Grille (or Café) in the Lower Lobby—where the gym and offices are found today—was designed in "Early American" fashion. The Grille proved a popular and quiet place for lunch and featured live music at night.

BUILDING A BETTER PARKER HOUSE

The Omni Parker House that visitors know today looks nothing like the five-story "New Marble Building" opened by Harvey Parker on October 8, 1855. In 1860, only five years after opening, the entrepreneur made a six-story addition to his hotel; another wing was added three years later. By 1866 he was able to purchase a narrow lot on Tremont, which adjoined his rear buildings, and added two floors to the School Street annex. Following two decades of negotiations, sales, and financial success, Parker had not yet fulfilled his personal dream for the Parker House. Still, he had substantially enlarged his original structure, eventually expanding the hotel over 41,400 square feet of land—the bulk of the city lot bordered by Tremont, School, and Bosworth streets and Chapman Place.

On May 31, 1884, Parker died at the age of seventy-nine; he was buried in Mount Auburn Cemetery, the "permanent home" of many of Boston's most prestigious people. By the time of his death, Parker was as famous as they come: the Maine farm boy who had arrived in Boston almost penniless in 1825 had a net worth of $1,272,546.94 when he drew his last breath. Though Parker was survived by his wife of forty-five years, Julia Ann, there was no heir-apparent to take the helm of his hotel. Parker's original partner, John F. Mills, had already passed away, as had Parker's two sons (one died at the age of seven, and the other was lost at sea at twenty-four). Hence, Parker's will granted $100,000 to Boston's Museum of Fine Arts (*see story on page 88*) and leased the Parker House to his later partners, Edward O. Punchard and Joseph H. Beckman.

The building was expanded soon after Parker's death, when Punchard and Beckman added a new wing, an eight-story annex, and elaborate exterior decorations. Roxbury grocer Joseph Reed Whipple, who had worked under the supervision of Parker's first partner, John F. Mills, took over in 1891. Though Whipple died in 1912, the J.R. Whipple Corporation bought the hotel from the Trustees of the Parker Estate in 1925. To the horror of many, they demolished Harvey Parker's old marble palace and built in its stead the "new" Parker House—essentially, the one we know today—which opened on May 12, 1927. (One wing remained open during construction, allowing Parker's to maintain its designation as America's "longest continuously operating hotel.")

Designed by G. Henri Desmond of Desmond & Lord architects, this 1927 version was believed by many contemporaries to be more beautiful than its predecessor. Built fourteen stories high, with polished Quincy granite on the exterior, it featured lush, ornamented public chambers with oak paneling, artfully plastered ceilings, crystal chandeliers, bronze-detailed doors, and eight hundred guest rooms.

Glenwood Sherrard took the helm of the Parker House in 1933, during the height of the Great Depression *(see story on page 92)*. In 1968, the historic hotel was acquired by the beloved Dunfey family, owners of nearly a dozen hotels *(see story on page 94)*. In 1975, the Dunfeys entered an agreement with Aer Lingus which enabled them to begin a multimillion-dollar renewal plan at the Parker House. When the Dunfeys purchased Omni Hotels in the 1980s—a chain of some forty properties—the Omni Parker House was designated the "flagship" of their upscale hotels. By 1996, Robert B. Rowling and his TRT Holdings, Inc., of Dallas, Texas, acquired Omni Hotels/ North America, bringing an even greater budget for new facilities and restoration.

As might be expected, changes in ownership inevitably brought physical changes at the Parker House. The hotel's basement area, once home to a billiard room, was supplanted by eateries like the English Grille Room and the first incarnation of The Last Hurrah, before it became the current fitness center (The Last Hurrah Bar is now located on street level off the main lobby). The mezzanine-level lobby lounge, landing, and reading library evolved into today's cozy Parker's Bar. An old banquet hall became the contemporary Press Room. The venerable Revere Room was updated into Café Tremont, which was adapted into a lobby-level meeting space called the Kennedy Room. And the 1935 Rooftop Terrace, closed in 1969, now hosts special functions. Bowing to modern needs for space, the eight hundred guest chambers of 1927 were restructured into 551 larger, uniquely shaped rooms and suites.

In 2008, the Omni Parker House returned to its original splendor thanks to a $30 million restoration that blended historic charm with modern-day amenities and comforts. Soothing hues, richly colored fabrics, custom cherry furnishing, and well-polished heirlooms brought warm memories of the old into the 530 guestrooms and 21 deluxe suites. Extending its operations in its third new century, the Omni Parker House began providing 24-hour complimentary health club services, 24-hour guest room dining, complimentary wireless Internet access in all common areas, and a professional concierge staff.

Harvey Parker and the MFA

This marble bust of Harvey D. Parker was created in Rome, Italy, by sculptor John Perry (1845-after 1879). The sculpture was a gift of Mrs. Hiram Whittington to the Museum of Fine Arts, Boston.

The Museum of Fine Arts, Boston, was opened to great acclaim in 1876—the year of the nation's centennial. Originally housed in a grand structure in Copley Square (then known as "Art Square"), the institution depended on the kindness of others for its ever-increasing collections.

The MFA's early Print Department included both ancient and modern works—bequests from diverse sources including the Boston Athenaeum, the late Senator Charles Sumner, Ednah Dow Cheney, several publishing houses, and a variety of artists and friends. But at its core was the precious Gray Collection, some 6,000 prints that were deposited there by Harvard College. No one but the Curator was allowed to handle Gray Collection prints, though visitors could arrange appointments to view pieces with the Curator present.

Boston's original Museum of Fine Arts opened in what is now known as Copley Square in 1876. In 1909, the museum moved to its present location on Huntington Avenue. This color postcard of the old MFA dates from the early twentieth century.

When the Gray Collection was subsequently pulled by Harvard, elation turned to dismay. But a stroke of luck saved the day—as well as the fledgling art museum's print collection. As one writer later observed, the MFA Print Department was "Saved From Extinction by Parker House Rolls."

But what happened? Following Harvey Parker's death in 1884, his estate bequeathed $100,000 to the MFA. Museum trustees invested the funds, hoping to eventually use interest income to replenish their print losses. That scenario came to pass in 1897, when $45,000 from The Harvey D. Parker Fund was used to purchase the newly available print collection of New York financier Henry F. Sewall (1816-95).

The Sewall Collection filled the MFA's needs perfectly. It was an impressive array of 23,000 etchings, engravings, lithographs, and other prints by the likes of Dürer, Rembrandt, Goya, Schongauer, and Hogarth. It also included some duplicates, which MFA curators sold in order to purchase works by the talented and provocative illustrator, Aubrey Beardsley. Most importantly, it became the new core of prints at the MFA.

Over the years, the endowment that saved the MFA Print Department has been referred to as "The Harvey D. Parker Collection." It has led some to believe that the prints belonged to Parker, rather than the true scenario: that Parker's monies purchased the Sewall Collection.

Harvey Parker, however, does retain an artful presence at the MFA to this day. His bust, a 28-inch tall marble piece sculpted by John Perry in 1874, sits proudly in the Morse Study Room, where visitors can view works on paper that are in permanent storage.

Better times, better roads, lower fares . . . every thing has conspired to make domestic travel more enjoyable this summer. Go North or South, go East or West, but go somewhere in America.

Historic New England . . . gay, thrilling New York . . . Philadelphia, Cradle of Liberty . . . the romantic hospitable South and Southwest . . . Chicago . . . the National Parks . . . the Rockies and the Pacific Coast —it's a grand country, this America of yours, and this is the year to see it.

And wherever you travel, however you travel, be sure to stop at a recognized hotel, where you'll be certain of comfort, safety and service.

HOTELS.

PARKER HOUSE

EUROPEAN PLAN.

HARVEY D. PARKER & CO.,

BOSTON, MASS.

HARVEY D. PARKER.   JOSEPH
EDWARD O. PUNCHARD.

Welcome Festibal

— TO —

S. D. NICKERSON, S. W OF W. L. L.

ON HIS RETURN FROM EUROPE.

PARKER HOUSE,   OCTOBER 22, 1890.

THE BURNS CLUB.

89

ANNIVERSARY DINNER.

AT THE
PARKER HOUSE,
FRIDAY EVENING JANUARY 25th, 1856.

Evans & Plummer, Printers and Engravers, 116 Washington Street, Boston.

Parker House

BOSTON'S MOST FAMOUS HOTEL

Glenwood J. Sherrard, President and Managing Director

Mr. Whipple's Side Dish

For multi-millionaire J. Reed Whipple, "one" was apparently never enough. At the turn of the twentieth century, he owned two prize-winning thoroughbred horses, "Brandy" and "Soda." He ran three of Boston's finest hotels: The Parker House, the Hotel Touraine, and Young's Hotel. He had four handsome and tastefully furnished homes: one on Commonwealth Avenue in Boston, another at Valley View Farm (*see story on page 34*) in New Boston, New Hampshire, a third on Lowell Street in Lexington, Massachusetts, as well as his private home quarters at the Parker House.

And a persistent urban legend—passed on by word of mouth and occasional printed materials—is that Whipple's interest in having "more than one" also applied to the women in his life. The first was his wife, Rose Gay Higgins (known as "Lou"), and the second, his alleged mistress, Mary A. Morrill. As legend goes, the wife was kept in Boston while the mistress was conveniently couched at what was known as Shagbark Farm in Lexington.

The Facts: J. Reed Whipple took over the Parker House in 1891. In 1893, the 300-acre farm and mansion at 265 Lowell Street, Lexington, was acquired in the name of Thomas B. Morrill. Curiously, no Thomas B. Morrill is listed in any of the Lexington Town Directories or in the town's vital statistics—not in 1893, and not in the following two decades. Tom Morrill, it turns out, was one of Mary A. Morrill's older brothers. (Another of her brothers, James Gilman Morrill, purchased the Hartshorne House and meadows in Wakefield with J. Reed Whipple in 1890, as a place for James Morrill and a partner named Atwood to harvest ice.)

According to a variety of historic sources, including the 1998 Massachusetts Historical Commission report researched by Nancy S. Seasholes, the actual purchaser of the Lexington estate in 1893 was the chief proprietor of the Parker House. And the actual inhabitants of the luxurious home at its center? Miss Mary Adeline Morrill and Mr. J. Reed Whipple.

In 1895, J. Reed transferred ownership directly to Mary. Over the next eight years, the two improved Shagbark Farm, added English Revival style finishes to the home at its center, built a gorgeous Colonial Revival stable, expanded the barn, added a windmill and a hexagonal water tower—and renamed the estate Cedarcrest. Then in 1903, Whipple bought the mansion back from Morrill for one dollar, permitting her to live there as long as she liked, and giving it to her outright should he predecease her.

The Whipple/Morrill Homestead in Lexington: The property, circa 1910; the same view, 2013; mansion closeup, 2013.

During the years in Lexington, Whipple used the extensive acreage at Cedarcrest to supply his Boston hotels—a small-scale version of his massive operation at Valley View Farm in New Hampshire. He raised hens and hogs and even one hundred head of cattle at Cedarcrest, then shipped produce both to his hotels and to Winning Farm in Woburn, another Whipple property that he used to stable his thoroughbred horses.

Whipple died on June 15, 1912, and was buried in New Boston, New Hampshire, overlooking his Valley View Farm. Miss Mary A. Morrill was listed as one of the attendees of his funeral at the New Old South Church in Boston. Shortly thereafter, Mary sold the Lexington property she had just legally inherited. She died fifteen years later, on March 29, 1927, and is buried at Woodlawn Cemetery in Everett, Massachusetts.

The Fuzzy History and Hearsay: Just because J. Reed and Mary owned and shared Shagbark/Cedarcrest, of course, does not necessarily mean they were lovers.

Still, the Whipple-Morrill love story has been hand-written in personal reminiscences, printed in Lexington newspaper articles and historic commission reports, and discussed for decades—especially by residents of the Fairlawn Nursing Home, which operated on this Lowell Street site during the second half of the twentieth century.

The essence of the popular tale is that Mary Morrill was a cashier at the Parker House, and J. Reed Whipple's wife was an invalid, confined to their Parker House residence. Alternate versions of the story say Mrs. Whipple remained at their Commonwealth Avenue mansion and that she simply refused to give J. Reed a divorce. Whatever the situation, Mr. Whipple fell in love with his cashier Mary, and set her up in their Lexington love nest. When Whipple took the property back into his own name in 1903, it may have been because the affair was going sour, or to avoid suspicious behavior or litigious events.

The Missing Pieces: Sadly, over the past century and a half, the vast majority of Parker House records, both personal and business, have been lost to fires, renovations, and mistaken housecleaning. Hence, if documents existed confirming that Mary A. Morrill was a cashier at the Parker House, that J. Reed's wife Rose was an invalid confined to their Boston home, that Rose refused J. Reed a divorce, and if, indeed, the Morrill-Whipple love affair took place, those tangible records have long since disappeared.

The Morrill of this story? You just never know for sure!

This sketch of J. Reed Whipple depicts him as contemporaries described him: a short, stout, dapper, eminently successful and wealthy businessman, and a determined character.

Glenwood Sherrard

In the early days of the Great Depression, the Parker House found itself in dire financial trouble. The J. R. Whipple Corporation was on its way out, and the Atlantic National Bank foreclosed on the historic hotel's mortgage. Hence, when the First National Bank acquired the Atlantic National Bank, it acquired the Parker House as well.

Then along came Glen Sherrard.

Born in Dorchester, Massachusetts, in 1895, Glenwood J. Sherrard began apprenticing in hotels across the U.S. at the

Glen Sherrard in 1940

tender age of fourteen. After serving in the U.S. Army from 1917-19, then marrying Jessie Lumsden in 1924, Sherrard moved to Bermuda, where he assumed the post of managing director and president of the Hamilton Hotel. When Boston came calling, however, Sherrard was eager to return to his home turf.

In February of 1933, the newly-formed G.J. Sherrard Company relieved the National Bank of its historic hotel, and took ownership of two buildings: the spanking new 14-story Parker House structure, built in 1927, and the old 10-story annex that stood behind it, on Chapman Place and Bosworth Street. The purchase was assessed at $3,300,000, almost half of which was listed as land value alone.

In the early years, Sherrard fulfilled Boston's hope that the Parker House could be revived and brought back to its former glory. Despite the continuing Depression, both the hotel and Sherrard prospered. Starting in 1934, he began taking over management of other properties, including the Hotel Bellevue and the Somerset in Boston, followed by the Eastern Slope Inn in North Conway, New Hampshire.

During centennial festivities for the Parker House—which were mistakenly celebrated in 1956*—President Eisenhower sent Sherrard and the hotel staff a congratulatory telegram, ending, "As the meeting place for many businesses, social and charitable groups, you have contributed to the life of your community and helped make Boston one of the most attractive metropolitan centers in our land. Best wishes to you all as you enter your second hundred years of service."

Glenwood Sherrard died in 1958. A decade without his leadership was at least part of the reason the Parker House again fell into hard times. A long-time employee remembered that Sherrard's well-meaning son, Andrew, picked up many of the day-to-day operations, but made bad business decisions—aggravated by his personal struggle with addiction

View down Tremont Street, as seen from a Parker House window, 1927

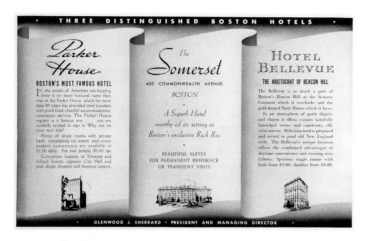

In this magazine ad from 1936-37, Sherrard advertised the Boston hotels he managed, including the Parker House, "Boston's Most Famous Hotel," and the Bellevue, "The Aristocrat of Beacon Hill."

and his naïve generosity. In 1968, ten years after Glen's death, his widow Jessie sold the tired old hotel to the Dunfey Family Corporation for a reported $5,000,000. Though other offers were made, she chose to sell "to people in the hotel business."

Glenwood Sherrard's final resting place is at Forest Hills Cemetery, Jamaica Plain. Marked by a small, flat, hard-to-find marker, it's a stone's throw away from one of the most popular pilgrimage sites at the cemetery: the grave of playwright Eugene O'Neill.

* *By 1927, when the first full-length book about Parker House history was published, the opening of the hotel was regularly listed as October 8, 1856. As commonly happens, that date was repeated article after article, story after story, and press release after press release throughout the twentieth century. Our recent research in newspapers of the era shows that the actual opening date was October 8, 1855—a year earlier. It appears that the error was a result of newspaper advertising customs of the mid-nineteenth century. Beginning several weeks before the actual opening, Harvey Parker ran a small classified ad announcing his marvelous new hotel would be opening "October 8." Problem is, the same ad continued to run in Boston newspapers long after October 8, 1855, well into the first half of 1856. Chances are, some researcher read the ads in an 1856 newspaper, thinking they referred to October 8 of that year, rather than the former.*

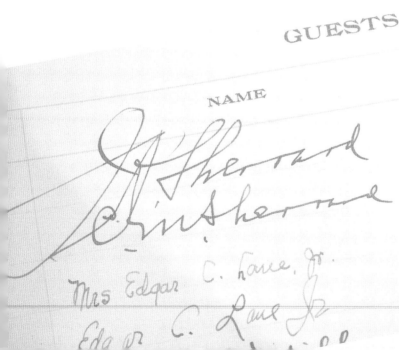

GUESTS

NAME

The final resting place of Glenwood J. Sherrard at Forest Hillls Cemetery, Jamaica Plain

Sherrard's signature, from a guestbook

The Dunfey Era

The Dunfeys were personal friends and political allies of Martin Luther King, Jr., and his family. Here Coretta Scott King dedicates the Martin Luther King Room at the Parker House in 1977.

94

The family credited with saving the old Parker House in the late 1960s was the Dunfeys of New Hampshire. Father Leroy opened a variety store-turned-luncheonette in Lowell, Massachusetts, in the 1930s, then helped his sons expand their business careers with a seacoast clam stand in Hampton Beach, New Hampshire, in 1945. The success of that enterprise enabled them to purchase and open other businesses—and ultimately to build a hotel empire that included Omni Hotels, the Royal Orleans Hotel in New Orleans, the Biltmore Plaza Hotel in Rhode Island, and Berkshire Place, New York City.

After buying their first real hotel in 1958 and founding the Dunfey Family Corporation, the five brothers—Jack, Bud, Bob, Walter, and Jerry—acquired various other properties throughout New England, including several existing hotels and motor inns that bore the prestigious Sheraton name. A second strategy—that of targeting struggling hotels in need of renovation that they could buy inexpensively—led to their purchase of the financially ailing Parker House from the Sherrards in 1968.

The Dunfey Family toasts founder Harvey Parker during 120th anniversary celebrations at the Parker House in 1976.

Boston Mayor Raymond Flynn is honored by Roy Dunfey at the Parker House.

The Dunfey clan not only rejuvenated and "reinvented" the Parker House as a historic/contemporary destination of choice, but also laid claim to its illustrious intellectual history. Inspired by the nineteenth century Saturday Club, they founded the New England Circle in 1974. In these unique and purposeful gatherings, business people could listen to community activists, academics could talk with hotel chambermaids, and refugees could be heard by political leaders, all with the intent of advancing civil and civic dialogue that could lead to constructive community change.

That kind of inclusive progressive politics extended to the Dunfey brothers' involvement in the Democratic Party and their support of a number of causes, including the Civil Rights movement. Among their close allies and personal friends were the families of John F. Kennedy and Martin Luther King, Jr. The Dunfeys expanded their work into international issues and contributed to peaceful resolutions in both South Africa and Northern Ireland—a move that was reflected in the name change of their popular forum from New England Circle to Global Citizens Circle.

"Our family regarded the Parker House as the centerpiece of their business and their interests in political and international issues," explains Will Dunfey, nephew of the

five brothers. "As a hotel renowned in the U.S. and beyond, the Parker House became a symbol of our family's move from a regional to a national and international hotel chain. The Parker House also was home for two of the Dunfey brothers for over a decade, was the site for many of our family celebrations, and remains the gathering place of choice for family visiting Boston to this day."

The Dunfeys also invented The Last Hurrah, a popular restaurant/pub that began downstairs and continues to this day as a street level bar, on the corner of Tremont and School. Will Dunfey recalls, "The first major event in The Last Hurrah quite appropriately celebrated the publication of *Johnny We Hardly Knew Ye: Memories of John Fitzgerald Kennedy*, by JFK's closest aides, Dave Powers and Kenny O'Donnell. The book party attracted figures from the Kennedy administration and other prominent political leaders from Massachusetts, including an infrequent public appearance of (retired) Speaker of the House John McCormack."

It's no wonder that the Dunfeys and the Dunfey Era at the Parker House have long been remembered and loved by Greater Bostonians.

The Dunfeys were longtime friends and supporters of the political Kennedy clan. Here, Eileen (Sr. Julie), Jack, and Bud Dunfey flank young Senator Edward Kennedy at the podium.

1. Cambodian survivor Arn Chorn Pond receives an award from singer/
   activist Harry Belafonte.

2. Among the prestigious doers and thinkers who attended the Dunfey's
   New England Circle gatherings were Richard Goodwin and his wife
   Doris Kearns, 1981.

3. Social and human rights activist Bianca Jagger with Jack Dunfey, 1982.

4. Eleanor Dunfey and Bob Dunfey, Sr., with the first female President of
   Ireland, Mary Robinson.

5. Jerry Dunfey with Elma Lewis and Muhammad Ali, circa 1980.

6. Civil Rights activist Julian Bond with Bob Dunfey, 1975.

7. Boston Symphony Orchestra conductor Seiji Ozawa with Jerry and
   Roy Dunfey, 1980.

SPECTRAL EVIDENCE

Though room furnishings, decor, utilities, and services have always been upgraded and fitted to the tastes and needs of each era, gracious hospitality and an attentive manner—initiated by Harvey Parker in 1855—have remained a constant at the historic Omni Parker House.

In a way, Harvey Parker himself has remained a constant at his world-famous hotel and restaurant. He has, that is, if you believe in spectral evidence.

"I first heard about the ghost of Harvey Parker when I began working here in 1941," explained a longtime bellman, the now-deceased John Brehm, in a 1992 *Boston Globe* interview. "They used to say he roamed the halls on the tenth floor annex. There were many stories, but one in particular happened around 1950. An elderly woman guest insisted she saw an apparition outside room 1078. At first it was a misty apparition in the air, then it turned toward her. She said it was a heavy-set older man with a black moustache. He just looked at her, then faded away. She came downstairs, a bit jittery, and security went up to the tenth floor. They checked it out, but reported they could find nothing."

Legend has it that a ghost may haunt one Parker House elevator.

To those who knew Harvey Parker, such sightings could hardly come as a shock. A perfectionist who kept his hands in every detail of his restaurant and hotel operations, he played the ultimate host to ordinary folks and world-famous guests. A host, it would seem, who could never really bring himself to leave.

Harvey wasn't the only ghost, either. There's the man, for example, who died in room 303 in 1949—and the inexplicable scent of whiskey that sometimes reappears in that chamber. Speaking of room 303, there's an apocryphal tale that's been making the rounds in recent years that needs to be ghost-busted: the Stephen King Thing.

You can find the story pretty much anywhere—in articles both on the web and in print, in books and lectures, and in numerous ghost tours of Boston. The essence of the tale, with varied embellishments, is that master of the macabre Stephen King (1) stays at the Omni Parker House when he comes to Boston for his beloved Red Sox games and (2) that he based his short-story-turned-film called *1408* on ghostly tales of Parker House room 303.

It's true that *1408* is King's own twist on the classic "Ghostly Room at the Inn" story. It's also true that in this horror tale, protagonist Mike Enslin is a writer who spends the night in a chamber where 42 deaths have occurred over 68 years, as research for his non-fiction book, *Ten Nights in Ten Haunted Hotel Rooms*. And no one is denying that room 303 at the Parker House has a long history of alleged hauntings. But are they connected?

We decided to go the source for the official answer. "It's just a rumor," explains King's assistant, Marsha DeFilippo. "And he doesn't stay at the Parker House when he's in Boston."

Sic transit gloria mundi.

There's also the mystery of the Number One elevator in the main building. Over the years, that elevator was periodically called to the third floor: the chime rang, the elevator car stopped, the doors opened, but no one was there. Ever. This allegedly happened hundreds of times and was checked—with no results—on dozens of occasions. Some suspected it was the ghost of Charles Dickens, who stayed on the third floor of the old Parker House in 1867 and 1868. Others think it might have been Charlotte Cushman, who lived in the Dickens suite in the 1870s. The fact is, it could have been any of a horde of legendary visitors. Remember, after all, the words of Dr. Oliver Wendell Holmes, in his poem, "At The Saturday Club."

Such guests! What famous names
its record boasts, Whose owners
wander in the mob of ghosts!

Seamus Says

As a kid growing up in a poor section of Dorchester, little Seamus (Gaelic for "James") Murphy knew nothing about the Parker House. He never went there, never ate there, and really didn't think about it at all.

By the year of the American Bicentennial, however, Seamus found himself searching for a summer job. Thanks to a friend who worked in housekeeping at the Parker House, the teenager came in for an interview. "I'll never forget first seeing that magnificent lobby and the leather chairs," he remembers. He also recalls his initial hire as a seasonal houseman, "and because it was 1976, we wore colonial outfits!"

Seamus never imagined he'd remain on the staff of the Parker House, but he did—working initially as an overnight bellman, while he attended high school and college.

He never imagined he would continue on at the Parker House for decades thereafter, as a bellman, a bell captain, and finally as Manager of Guest Services. Seamus is happy to tell guests about the famous folks he's met over those years, from Ed Asner, Henry Kissinger, and Jesse Owens to Ricky Nelson, Vincent

Price, and Bill Clinton. All those celebrities paled, however, compared to his close encounters with Hollywood paramour, Ann-Margret—who arrived with flowing scarf, big sunglasses, and a small dog, and promised him she'd "never forget the name Seamus!"

But most of all, what Seamus Murphy never imagined is that he would meet one of the legendary Parker House ghosts.

"I had heard stories about ghosts here, but in twenty-two years as a bellman never had an experience of my own. Around 2010, though, there was an event....you know the *Saturdays with Seamus* program I give?" he asks, referring to the delightfully informative and anecdotal talks he gives on Parker House and Boston history.

"Well, we were in the Longfellow Room, and I usually speak from a podium, but there was none there. I went to the storage room on the mezzanine level and heard a gruff voice yell out, 'What do you want??!!'

"I thought it was a houseman at first. But there was nobody on the floor. Nobody at all. And the voice sounded just like a bell captain that used to work here. He had been a drinker, and sometimes after work hours, he'd go off to some bar, then wander back into the hotel late at night, and hide out here in some sliding closet.

"So I thought it was probably him. Yeah, it really sounded exactly like him. Except for that fact that he's dead."

Was it a ghost? Seamus Murphy will never know for sure.

But perhaps someone simply mistook his current title as Manager of *Ghost* Services.

JOHN PARKER, LORD BORINGDON.
1784.

Parker House
Boston

THE PARKER COAT OF ARMS

Perched above the School Street entrance of the Omni Parker House is a large heraldic shield. What appears to be the Parker Family Coat of Arms has graced this spot since the "new" Parker House opened in 1927. Over the decades, the original monotone shield has become more colorful and its setting more ornate.

A description of the coat of arms in traditional heraldic terms would run roughly like this: The *field*, or background, of the shield is dominated by a stag staring straight at the viewer, while the *supporters* to the left and right are a dog and another stag. The *coronet* above the shield is a hand holding a laurel branch skyward, while the *crest* above that is a pine cone. Below the shield stretches a *motto*, the Latin phrase, "Fideli Certa Merces," which translates as, "To the faithful there is certain reward."

For more than a century, this symbol has adorned a variety of Parker House items in addition to the School Street entrance—from menus and matchbooks to stationery and stamps. That the Parker Family Coat of Arms exists is much easier to ascertain than what it actually means.

Research into English heraldry shows that there have been dozens, if not hundreds, of Parker Family shields throughout Britain's long history. That comes as no surprise, since "Parker" has long been a common surname. This particular Parker coat of arms is nearly identical to that of John Parker, who was awarded the title of Lord Boringdon by King George III on May 18, 1784 (that's the same King George who lost the colonies in American's War of Independence). John Parker commissioned the building of the Morley Arms, a pub in Plymouth, England, in 1824—where his coat of arms still hangs in the bar today.

But what about Harvey? Genealogical studies suggest that Harvey's family descended from one Thomas Parker, who traveled from England to Lynn, Massachusetts in 1635, arriving in the New World on the ship *Susan and Ellen*. That Parker ancestor was one of six church members who incorporated the town of Reading as a separate entity from Lynn. But what the relationship was between Thomas Parker and Lord Boringdon's Parkers is not in the least bit clear.

What *is* clear is that Harvey adapted the Parker coat of arms—no matter whether he inherited or co-opted the old design. The one significant difference between the Parker House shield and the old English original it mirrors is the object at the very top. Parker's coat of arms is topped by what appears to be a pine cone. Not so coincidentally, the white pine cone is the official state flower of Maine, while the eastern white pine is that state's official tree. Maine itself is nicknamed "The Pine Tree State."

When Maine was a District of the Commonwealth of Massachusetts—a status that lasted from colonial times until 1820—lumbering was a mainstay of the state economy. The lumber was lost to Massachusetts when Maine declared its independence. But the Bay State's indebtedness to Maine's precious natural resource is forever reflected in the topmost accoutrement of the 1798 Massachusetts State House: a gilded pine cone sits atop the golden dome.

Harvey D. Parker was born in Maine in 1805—meaning that he, like the forests of eastern white pines, was part of Maine when Maine was part of Massachusetts. So is Harvey's Maine heritage why the coat of arms at the Parker House features a pine cone at its pinnacle? We may never know for sure.

Facing page (top, left to right): The John Parker, Lord Boringdon, family crest as depicted in 1784; the Parker Crest as shown on a 1902 Parker's Restaurant menu; and the Parker Family Crest at the School Street entrance of the hotel.

About the Author

When not working as the official House Historian for the Omni Parker House, SUSAN WILSON spends her time as a writer, photographer, lecturer, educator, and consultant based in Cambridge, Waltham, and Wellfleet, Massachusetts. The recipient of a B.A. and M.A. in history from Tufts University, she gained early recognition as a regular contributor on the arts, music, and Boston history for the *Boston Globe* from 1978 through 1996. Her recent books include *Boston Sites and Insights* (Beacon Press, 2004), *The Literary Trail of Greater Boston* (Commonwealth Editions, 2005), *Garden of Memories* (Forest Hills Educational Trust, 1998), and *A Brief History of Beacon Press* (Beacon Press, 2003). She was the co-author of *Boston and the American Revolution* (Boston National Historical Park, 2000) and contributing essayist and editor of *Symphony Hall, The First 100 Years* (Boston Symphony Orchestra, 2000). The author of countless thematic walking tours and talks as well as historic signage on Boston Common and the Boston Harborwalk, she also served as project director for the Maritime Museum at Battery Wharf.

As co-director of Melodic Vision, Wilson also creates and performs multimedia pieces on various cultural, social, and historic topics. Visit her websites at www.susanwilsonphoto.com/books and www.melodicvision.com.

About the Designer

After earning a B.A. in Art History and Fine Arts from the University of Michigan, PAT NIESHOFF established her design studio, which has been based in Lexington, Massachusetts, for nearly two decades. Book design has always held a special interest for Pat, and the original Omni Parker House booklet, published in 2001, was a favorite project. Pat has collaborated with Susan Wilson on a variety of historic publications over the past fifteen years, including the book, *Garden of Memories*, as well as colorful guides for The Boston Women's Heritage Trail and Tufts University. Pat's long-time design colleagues, Heather Shaw and Kathleen Sayre, also worked on this newly-expanded, lavishly-illustrated Omni Parker House book, and provided invaluable design contributions. View more of Pat's design work—both interactive and print—at www.nieshoffdesign.com.

FAMOUS OMNI PARKER HOUSE GUESTS

Charles Francis Adams ❦ Jerry Adams ❦ Ben Affleck ❦ Louis Agassiz ❦ Alan Alda ❦ Anthony Athanas ❦ Red Auerbach ❦ Thomas Bailey Aldrich ❦ Muhammad Ali ❦ American Suffrage Association ❦ Oliver Ames ❦ The Atlantic Club ❦ The Beach Boys ❦ Harry Belafonte ❦ Alexander Graham Bell ❦ Barbie Benton ❦ Sarah Bernhardt ❦ The Bird Club ❦ Edwin Booth ❦ John Wilkes Booth ❦ David Bowie ❦ William ("Hopalong Cassidy") Boyd ❦ Michelle Branch ❦ Jackson Brown ❦ John Brown ❦ William Jennings Bryan ❦ James Carroll ❦ Jimmy Carter ❦ Rosalynn Carter ❦ Willa Cather ❦ Neville Chamberlain ❦ Charles, Prince of Wales ❦ Rufus Choate ❦ The Clash ❦ Grover Cleveland ❦ William Jefferson Clinton ❦ David Copperfield ❦ Bob Cousy ❦ Dave Cowens ❦ Joan Crawford ❦ James Michael Curley ❦ Charlotte Cushman ❦ Augustin Daly ❦ Richard Henry Dana, Jr. ❦ Felix O.C. Darley ❦ James Dean ❦ Charles Dickens ❦ Gerald Charles Dickens ❦ Mark Dickens ❦ Bob Dole ❦ Michael Dukakis ❦ John Sullivan Dwight ❦ Ralph Waldo Emerson ❦ Arthur Fiedler ❦ Annie Adams Fields ❦ James T. Fields ❦ David Hackett Fischer ❦ John F. Fitzgerald ❦ Fleetwood Mac ❦ Raymond Flynn ❦ Jane Fonda ❦ Gerald Ford ❦ John Kenneth Galbraith ❦ Isabella Stewart Gardner ❦ Judy Garland ❦ William Lloyd Garrison ❦ Richard Gebhart ❦ Rudy Giuliani ❦ Kelsey Grammer ❦ Ulysses S. Grant ❦ Grateful Dead ❦ Denyce Graves ❦ Marvelous Marvin Hagler ❦ Hall & Oates ❦ John Havlicek ❦ Nathaniel Hawthorne ❦ Kerry Healey ❦ Hugh Hefner ❦ Henry Lee Higginson ❦ Ho Chi Minh ❦ Oliver Wendell Holmes, Sr. ❦ Evander Holyfield ❦ Bob Hope ❦ Samuel Gridley Howe ❦ William Dean Howells ❦ John Hume ❦ William Morris Hunt ❦ John B. Hynes ❦ Henry Irving ❦ Ira Jackson ❦ Clara Louise Kellogg ❦

and more...

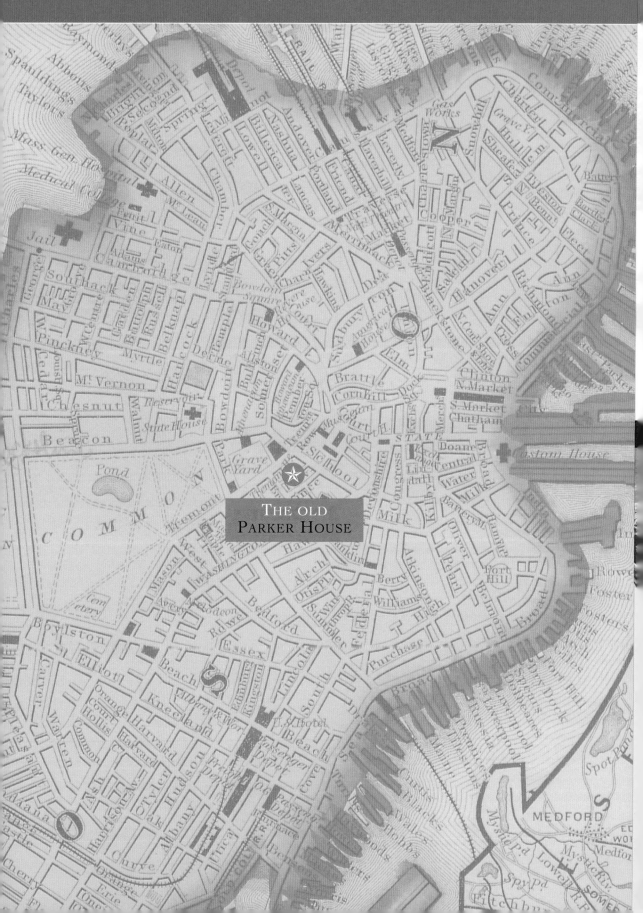

THE OLD
PARKER HOUSE

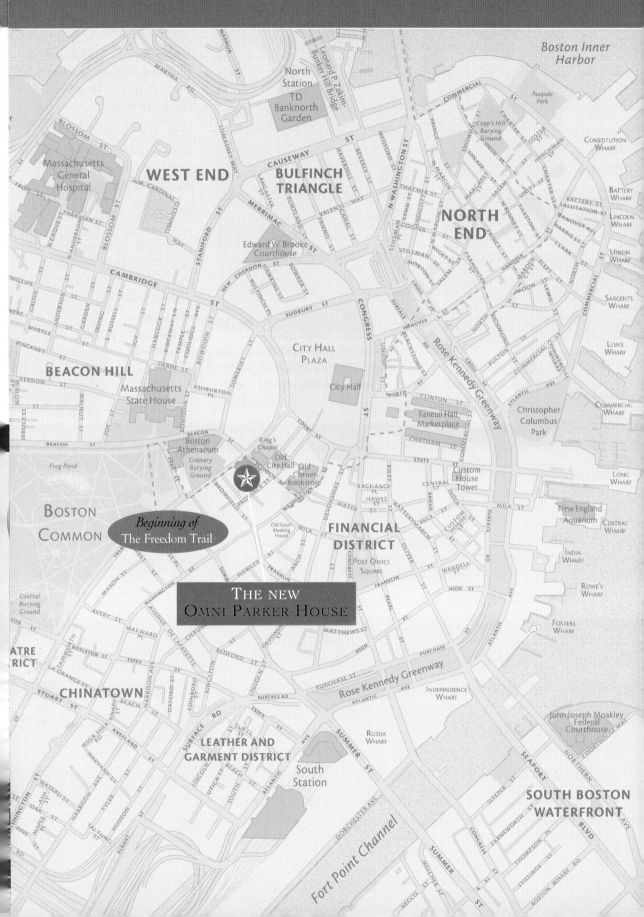

Edward Kennedy ❧ Eunice Kennedy ❧ John Fitzgerald Kennedy ❧ John Kerry ❧ BB King ❧ Coretta Scott King ❧ Don King ❧ Martin Luther King, Jr. ❧ Mel King ❧ Kiss ❧ Nick Lachey ❧ Emeril Lagasse ❧ Bernard Francis (Cardinal) Law ❧ Don Law ❧ Lennox Lewis ❧ Mary Todd Lincoln ❧ Henry Cabot Lodge ❧ John D. Long ❧ Alice Longfellow ❧ Henry Wadsworth Longfellow ❧ James Russell Lowell ❧ Yo-Yo Ma ❧ Nelson Mandela ❧ Richard Mansfield ❧ Bernard Margolis ❧ Ann-Margret ❧ Ziggy Marley ❧ Alexandra Marshall ❧ Johnny Mathis ❧ David McCullough ❧ George McGovern ❧ Thomas Menino ❧ Bette Midler ❧ Elizabeth Montgomery ❧ John Lothrop Motley ❧ Ricky Nelson ❧ Stevie Nicks ❧ Leonard Nimoy ❧ Charles Eliot Norton ❧ Paul O'Connell ❧ Jacques Offenbach ❧ Bobby Orr ❧ David Ortiz ❧ Jesse Owens ❧ Francis Parkman ❧ Deval Patrick ❧ Adelina Patti ❧ Benjamin Peirce ❧ Ross Perot ❧ Tom Petty ❧ Jon B. Platt ❧ Colin Powell ❧ William Prescott ❧ Prince of Joinville, son of King Louis Phillipe of France ❧ Vincent Price ❧ Wolfgang Puck ❧ Lou Rawls ❧ Rachael Ray ❧ Mary Robinson ❧ Mitt Romney ❧ Eleanor Roosevelt ❧ Franklin Delano Roosevelt ❧ Babe Ruth ❧ The Saturday Club ❧ Claudia Schiffer ❧ David Shiner ❧ Lydia Shire ❧ Dinah Shore ❧ Sargent Shriver ❧ Gypsy Smith ❧ Elizabeth Cady Stanton ❧ Roger Staubach ❧ Casey Stengel ❧ Charles Sumner ❧ William O. Taylor ❧ William Makepeace Thackery ❧ Luis Tiant ❧ Ellen Terry ❧ Henry David Thoreau ❧ Paul Tsongas ❧ Kathleen Turner ❧ Ted Turner ❧ Desmond Tutu ❧ George Wallace ❧ Samuel Gray Ward ❧ William Weld ❧ Adam ("Batman") West ❧ Edwin Percy Whipple ❧ Joseph Reed Whipple ❧ Jasper White ❧ Kevin White ❧ John Greenleaf Whittier ❧ The Who ❧ Ted Williams ❧ Woodrow Wilson ❧ Roger Wolcott ❧ Malcolm X ❧ Carl Yastrzemski ❧ Tom Yawkey

Such guests! What famous names its record boasts...
~ Oliver Wendell Holmes

Photo and Illustration Credits

Every effort has been made to credit and/or contact image sources for this book. Please contact us if there is an error or omission and we will correct the entry in future editions.

Courtesy the Alexander Graham Bell Family Papers, the U.S. Library of Congress Manuscript Division: page 12 (bottom)

Courtesy The Boston Herald: pages 41, 49 (top left), 60 (bottom left), 61 (top left)

Courtesy the Boston Public Library, Print Department: pages 31 (top), 43 (middle), 58, 60, 61 (bottom), 80

Courtesy the City of Boston Archives: page 62

Courtesy the Dunfey Family: pages 94, 95, 96 (top), 97

Courtesy the Franklin D. Roosevelt Presidential Library and Museum, U.S. National Archives: page 28

Courtesy The Illustrated London News, March 19, 1870: page 49 (bottom right)

Courtesy the John Fitzgerald Kennedy Library, President's Collection, Boston, Massachusetts: pages 56, 57 (all except Table 40)

Courtesy George Kyle, The Eighteen Fifties, Being a Brief account of School Street, The Province House, and the Boston Five Cents Savings Bank, Boston, 1926: page 15

Courtesy the Lexington Historical Society: page 90 (bottom left)

Courtesy the Museum of Fine Arts, Boston: page 88 (top)

Courtesy the U.S. National Archives: page 67 (bottom)

Courtesy the New Boston Historical Society, New Boston, New Hampshire: pages 34-35 (background), 35 (bottom left), 36 (all except bottom right), 37 (all except top right), 38 (all except top left), 39 (all except middle right), 91

Courtesy the Omni Parker House, Boston: cover (bottom), pages 9, 12, 14, 17, 18, 20, 25, 26, 31, 32, 49 (top middle), 63, 68, 71 (bottom left), 73 (middle), 75, 82, 83, 84, 87, 89, 90 (top), 92 (bottom), 93 (top and bottom left), 96 (bottom right), 99 (bottom), 101, 102 (middle), 103 (bottom)

Courtesy Thomas P. O'Neill III: pages 6-7

Courtesy Person + Killian Photography: pages 24, 40, 41

Courtesy the U.S. Library of Congress, Prints and Photographs Division: pages 12 (top), 22, 51 (top), 59, 67 (bottom), 72 (right)

Courtesy James W. Spring, Boston & the Parker House, J.R. Whipple Corporation, 1927 book: pages 48 (middle), 85, 90 (top), 103 (left)

Courtesy Tercentenary of the Founding of Boston, His Honor James M. Curley, Mayor: page 43 (top and map)

Courtesy the Willa Cather Pioneer Memorial and Educational Foundation, public domain image: page 53 (top)

Original copyrighted photos by Susan Wilson: 10, 23, 29, 31 (bottom), 34, 35 (right), 36 (bottom right), 37 (top right), 38 (top left), 39 (middle right), 48 (bottom left), 49 (top right), 54, 57 (Table 40), 70, 71 (bottom right), 73 (bottom right), 77, 90 (bottom middle and right), 93 (bottom right), 98, 99, 100, 102 (top right), 103 (right), 104 (with Susan Freundlich)

Courtesy Elsa Wilkens Photography: page 104 (bottom)

Public domain archival images courtesy the private collection of Susan Wilson: cover (top), pages 2, 10, 11, 13, 33 (top), 42, 45, 46 (bottom left), 47, 48 (top left), 49 (top right), 52 (bottom), 53 (bottom three), 55, 61 (top right), 65, 66, 67 (top), 79, 81, 88 (bottom), 92 (top), 102 (left)

Courtesy the Winiker Bands: pages 74, 76

Public domain images courtesy Wikimedia Commons: pages 46 (top), 51 (bottom), 52 (top), 69, 72 (left), 73 (top)

Famous Visitors Collage

(Inside front and back covers)

Original copyrighted photos by Susan Wilson: Jane Fonda, Yo-Yo Ma, Thomas Menino, Thomas P. O'Neill, Kathleen Turner.

Public domain archival images courtesy the private collection of Susan Wilson: Edwin Booth, John Wilkes Booth, Charles Dickens, Mary Baker Eddy, Ralph Waldo Emerson, Annie Adams Fields, James T. Fields, Isabella Stewart Gardner, William Lloyd Garrison, Oliver Wendell Holmes, Sarah Orne Jewett, Mary Todd Lincoln, Henry Wadsworth Longfellow, Ho Chi Minh, Glenwood Sherrard.

Courtesy the Dunfey Family: Harry Belafonte, Julian Bond, the Dunfey brothers, Arthur Fiedler with Dave Crohan, Richard and Doris Kearns Goodwin, Bianca Jagger with Jack Dunfey, Edward Kennedy, Coretta Scott King, Elma Lewis with Cassius Clay, Seiji Ozawa with Jerry and Roy Dunfey, Mary Robinson, Gloria Steinem.

Courtesy the City of Boston Archives: Larry Bird, Jimmy Carter, James Michael Curley, Michael and Kitty Dukakis, Raymond Flynn, Joseph Kennedy, Jr., John Kerry, Bernard Law, Robert Parrish, Paul Tsongas, Kevin White, Kevin White with Michael Dukakis, Michael Dukakis with Raymond Flynn, Geraldine Ferraro, John Kerry, Kitty Dukakis, and Edward Kennedy.

Courtesy the John Fitzgerald Kennedy Library, President's Collection, Boston, Massachusetts: John F. Kennedy, John F. Kennedy with Rose and Joseph Kennedy.

Courtesy the Office of the Governor of Massachusetts: Governor Deval Patrick, 2012, by Eric Haynes.

Courtesy the Omni Parker House, Boston: Harvey D. Parker, J. Reed Whipple.

Courtesy the U.S. Library of Congress, Prints and Photographs Division: Cassius Clay (Muhammad Ali), 1967, by staff photographer Ira Rosenberg from the *World Journal Tribune* collection; Ulysses S. Grant, from the Brady-Handy Collection;

Clara Louise Kellogg, circa 1855-1865, from the Brady-Handy Collection; Robert Todd Lincoln; Babe Ruth; drawing of Elizabeth Cady Stanton, at the Frederick Douglass home in Washington, D.C., from the Carol M. Highsmith Archive; Henry David Thoreau by Daniel Ricketson; Mark Twain from the Mathew Brady Collection; Edith Wharton; Malcolm X, 1964, by staff photographer Ed Ford, from the *New York World-Telegram & Sun* Collection.

Courtesy the U.S. National Archives: John Brown, Bill Clinton, Kelsey Grammer, B.B. King, Nelson Mandela, Jesse Owens, Woodrow Wilson.

Courtesy the Franklin D. Roosevelt Presidential Library and Museum, U.S. National Archives: Eleanor Roosevelt, Franklin D. Roosevelt.

Courtesy the archival collection of Martha S. Hassell: Charles Sumner.

Courtesy the Willa Cather Pioneer Memorial and Educational Foundation: Willa Cather, 1912, by Aime Dupont.

Public domain images courtesy Wikimedia Commons: Ben Affleck, 2009, Feed America; Ann-Margret, 1960s publicity photo; Alexander Graham Bell, circa 1914-19, by Moffett Studio, Library and Archives Canada; Sarah Bernhardt, circa 1878, by Paul Nadar; Judy Garland, undated publicity photo; Denyce Graves, 2009, by Chad J. McNeeley, U.S. Navy; Hugh Hefner, 1970 publicity photo, from *Playboy After Dark*; Bob Hope, 1940 publicity photo, from Hope's radio program, NBC radio; William Dean Howells, circa 1875-1882, by George Kendall Warren; Emeril Lagasse, undated, by Spc. Leah R. Burton, U.S. Army; Leonard Nimoy, 1968 publicity photo, from *Star Trek*, NBC Television; Jacques Offenbach, circa 1861-71, by Félix Nadar; Ted Williams, 1949, from *Baseball Digest*.

Courtesy the Winiker Bands: Bo Winiker, the Winiker Family Band.

INDEX

Abolition, 66–67

About the Farm (Whipple Company), 35

Adams, Charles Francis, 47

Adams, Gerry, 6

Adams, John, 16

Adams House, 17, 78

Aer Lingus airlines, 86

Affleck, Ben, 10

Agassiz, Louis, 47

Age of Innocence, The (Wharton), 52

Ali, Muhammad. *See* Clay, Cassius

Aloise, Adam, 8

American House, 17, 78

Ann-Margret, 10, 100

Anthony's Pier Four, 72

Appleman, Harry, 76

Architectural aspects, 78–87

Arlington Street Church, 79

Arn Chorn Pond, 97

Atlantic Monthly (magazine), 45, 47, 51

Atlantic National Bank, 92

"At the Saturday Club" (Holmes), 11, 99

Back Bay, 79

Ballou Hall, 79

Barnicle, Mike, 59

Bates College, 79

Beacon Hill, 54

Beatty, Jack, 58–59

Beckman, Joseph H., 78, 86

Belafonte, Harry, 97

Bell, Alexander Graham, 12

Bell, Mabel Gardiner Hubbard, 12

Bell Telephone Company, 12

Berkshire Place, 94

Bernhardt, Sarah, 10, 64, 69

Bisco family, 20

Bond, Julian, 97

Bonello, John, 26, 31

Booth, Edwin, 10, 64

Booth, John Wilkes, 10, 64–65

Booth, Junius, Jr., 64

Boston Athenaeum, 42, 44, 45, 47, 88

Boston City Hall (new), 62

Boston City Hall (old), 43, 58, 79

Boston Common, 14

Boston Consolidated Gas Company Building, 82

Boston Courier (newspaper), 67

Boston Cream Pie, 24–25, 33, 68

"Boston Day Parade," 43

Boston Evening Transcript (newspaper), 65

Boston Globe (newspaper), 5, 22, 51, 59, 83, 98

Boston Herald (newspaper), 61, 77

Boston Museum, 64

Boston Police Strike (1919), 7

Boston Post (newspaper), 21, 67, 69

Boston scrod, 26, 33

Boston Symphony Orchestra, 97

Boston Theatre, 10, 64

Boston Transcript (newspaper), 19

Boston University

    Huntington Theatre Company, 59

    Boston University Medical Center, 83

    Boston University Bridge, 82

    Boston University School of Oratory, 12

Boyd, William, 10

Boylston, Nicholas, 15

Boylston Hotel, 16

Brady, Matthew B., 67

Brehm, John, 70–71, 98

Brown, Julia Ann. *See* Parker, Julia Ann Brown

Bryant, Gridley James Fox, 78–81, 92

Bulfinch, Charles, 82

Burnham, Sophia, 20

Cather, Willa, 53

Cedarcrest estate, 90–91

Charles Street Jail, 79

Charlestown State Prison, 79

Chekijian, Yervant, 8

Cheney, Ednah Dow, 88

Child, Julia, 33

Child, Lydia Maria, 44

Christmas Carol, A (Dickens), 47, 68

Churchill, Winston, 29

Civil War (1861-1865), 7, 65, 67, 68

Clay, Cassius, 72, 97

Clemens, Samuel. *See* Twain, Mark

Clinton, William Jefferson "Bill," 10, 54, 62

Coat of arms, Parker, 102–103

Cocktails, 26–27

Codman, James, 22

Conant, Ben B., 20

Contes d'Hoffmann, Les (Offenbach opera), 30

Copley Square, 88

Copperfield, David, 72

Cottage Farm Bridge, 82

Cotto, Edward John "Eddie," 70–72

Crawford, Joan, 10

Crohan, David, 73

Curley, James Michael, 10, 29, 55, 58–62

Currency, Parker House private, 68

Cushman, Charlotte, 10, 64–65, 99

Daly, Augustin, 64

Dean, James, 10

DeFilippo, Marsha, 99

Desmond, G. Henri, 81–82

Desmond & Lord Architects, 81–83

Dever, Paul, 6

Dickens, Charles, 19, 44, 47–50, 53, 68, 99

Dickens, Gerald Charles, 68

Dickens Room (Omni Parker House), 48

Dock Square Parking Garage, 83

Dodge, Oliver H., 35–36

Dodge's Store, 37

Dorchester Bay Bridge, 82

Drury, Anna, 20

Drury, Luke, 20

Dukakis, Michael, 62

Dunfey, Bob, 94, 97

Dunfey, Bud, 94

Dunfey, Eleanor, 97

Dunfey, Jack, 94, 97

Dunfey, Jerry, 94, 97

Dunfey, Roy, 73, 75, 97

Dunfey, Ruth, 73, 75, 87

Dunfey, Walter, 94

Dunfey, Will, 96

Dunfey family, 6, 63, 71, 75, 77, 87, 94–97

Dunfey's Parker House, 63, 71, 75, 87, 94–97

See also Omni Parker House

Dupont, Aime, 53

Dutchess Divider, 31

Dwyer, Ruth, 5

Eagle Wing (ship), 22

Eddy, Mary Baker, 53

Eisenhower, Dwight D., 92

Emerson, Ralph Waldo, 10, 44–45, 47, 53

Emery, George F., 21

Escoffier, Auguste, 33

Faneuil Hall Marketplace, 25, 58

Fiedler, Arthur, 73

Fields, Annie Adams, 45, 50, 53

Fields, James T., 45, 47, 51, 53

First Church of Christ, Scientist, 53

Fitchburg Depot, 46

Fitzgerald, John "Honey Fitz," 55

Flay, Bobby, 33

Flynn, Raymond, 76

Ford's Theatre, 65

Forest Hills Cemetery, 93

Franklin, Benjamin, 14

Franklin D. Roosevelt Presidential Library and Museum, 28–29

Freedom Trail, 11, 59, 71

Fuller, Margaret, 44

Garland, Judy, 10, 73

Garrison, William Lloyd, 67

Georgas, Philip, 8, 76

George III, King of Britain, 102

Gilman, Arthur, 79

Gilman, Daniel and Fred, 35

Giuliani, Rudy, 62

Goodwin, Doris Kearns, 97

Goodwin, Richard, 97

Government Center, 62, 83

Grammer, Kelsey, 10

Grant, Ulysses S., 10, 54, 59

Graves, Denyce, 31

Gray Collection (MFA), 88

Great Depression, 92

Great Fire (1872), 7

Groom, Thomas, 68

Hamilton Hotel, 92

Hart, Claude M., 8, 81, 83

Harvard College, 14, 67, 88

Harvey D. Parker Collection, 88

Hasty Pudding Club, 29

Hathorn Hall, 79

Hawthorne, Nathaniel, 10, 16, 42, 44, 47, 53

Healey, Kerry, 62

Hefner, Hugh, 72

History of Christian Science (Cather/Milmine), 53

Ho Chi Minh, 7, 10, 31, 33

Hollis, Vesti, 81

Holmes, Oliver Wendell, Sr., 11, 16, 44, 46, 47, 54, 68, 99

Hopkins, John, 8

Horticultural Hall, 42, 79

Hotel Bellevue, 92

Hotels, beginning of, 17

Hotel Touraine, 34, 90

Houghton Mifflin Company, 45, 53

Houses, lodging, 17

Howard Athenaeum, 64

Howe, Julia Ward, 67

Howells, William Dean, 51

Hubbard, Mabel Gardiner. *See* Bell, Mabel Gardiner Hubbard

Hunt, John E., 18, 21

Huntington Theatre Company, 59

Innocents Abroad, The (Twain), 51

Irving, Henry, 64

Jagger, Bianca, 97

James, Henry, 53

Jefferson, Thomas, 66

Jeffery, Laurence, 8

Jewett, Sarah Orne, 53

Johnny We Hardly Knew Ye (Powers/O'Donnell), 96

Jones, Edith Newbold. *See* Wharton, Edith

Joutz, Rainer, 8

J.R. Whipple Corporation, 34–36, 38–9, 81, 86

Julius Caesar (Shakespeare), 65

Kellogg, Clara Louise, 21–22

Kennedy, Edward M. "Teddy," 63, 96

Kennedy, Jacqueline Bouvier, 55–56

Kennedy, John Fitzgerald "Jack," 10, 40, 54–56, 96

Kennedy, Kara, 63

Killian, Laurén, 40

King, Coretta Scott, 94

King, Martin Luther, Jr., 94, 96

King, Stephen, 98–99

King's Chapel, 14, 15, 42

Knapp, Michael, 8

Lagasse, Emeril, 31, 33

Last Hurrah, The (O'Connor), 58–59, 61

LePage, Al, 49

Lewis, Elma, 97

Life (magazine), 55

Lillie, Lloyd, 58

Lincoln, Abraham, 65–67

Lincoln, Mary Todd, 67

Lincoln, Robert Todd, 67

Literary associations, 44–53
   See also specific writers

Literary Club, 45

Little, Malcolm. See X, Malcolm

Logan, Edward Lawrence, 43

Logan Airport, 43, 83

Longfellow, Henry Wadsworth, 10, 44, 47, 68

Lord, Israel Pierre, 81–82

Lowell, Amy, 44, 46

Lowell, James Russell, 47

Lumber industry, 103

Ma, Yo-Yo, 10

MacMillan, Beau, 33

Magazine Club, 45

Mansfield, Richard, 64

Marble Heart, The (Selby), 65

Martin Luther King Room (Omni Parker House), 76, 94

Mary Baker Eddy (Cather), 53

Mason, Richard, 8

Massachusetts Bay Colony, 13

Massachusetts Horticultural Society, 42

Massachusetts State House, 19, 54, 78, 79

Maynes, Michael, 22

McCormack, John, 96

McCrindle, James, 8

McIntosh, Robert, 8

Memories of a Hostess (Fields), 50

Mercantile Wharf Building, 79

Mico, John, 16, 19

Midler, Bette, 76–77

Mills, John F., 18, 86

Milmine, Georgina, 53

Mission Hill, 70

Morley Arms (Plymouth, England), 102

Morrill, James Gilman, 90

Morrill, Mary Adeline, 90, 91

Morrill, Thomas B., 90

Moscardelli, Al, 73

Mount Auburn Cemetery, 23, 86

Mulligan, Alice, 83

Murphy, Seamus, 100

Murtha, John, 5, 8, 77

Museum of Fine Arts, Boston, 22–23, 86, 88

My Antonia (Cather), 53

Nadar, Félix, 30

Nathan, Norma, 77

National Theatre, 78

Nesbitt, Henrietta, 28–29

New Boston (New Hampshire), 34

New Boston Creamery, 37

New Boston Fairgrounds, 39

New Boston Historical Society, 35

New England Circle, 6, 96

New England Conservatory of Music, 75

New Old South Church, 91

Nguyen Sinh Cung. *See* Ho Chi Minh

Nicks, Stevie, 10

North American Review (magazine), 44, 45

Norton, Clement, 54–55

O'Connell, Paul, 31

O'Connor, Edwin, 58, 60

O'Donnell, Kenny, 96

Offenbach, Jacques, 30

Old Corner Bookstore, 15, 45–47, 51, 53

Old State House (Massachusetts), 78

Omni Hotels & Resorts, 8, 94

Omni Parker House
    architectural aspects, 78–87
    bands, 74–77
    bars, 59–62, 73, 85, 96
    chefs, 31–33
    coat of arms, 102–103
    farm and creamery, 34–39
    founding of, 10–11
    ghosts, 98–100
    interiors, 84–85
    literary associations, 44–53
    neighborhood, 13–16, 42
    150th anniversary, 25, 68
    political clientele, 54–63
    private currency, 68
    theatrical associations, 64–69
    See also specific individuals; specific topics

O'Neil, William J., 59

O'Neill, Thomas P., III, 6–7

O'Neill, Thomas "Tip," 6–7, 73

O Pioneers! (Cather), 53

Ortiz, David, 10

"Our Famous Men" (Emery), 21

Ozawa, Seiji, 97

Paris (Maine), 20

Parker, Harvey D., 10, 16, 64, 79
    background, 20–23
    death, 86, 88
    early career, 18–19
    ghost of, 98
    and Museum of Fine Arts, Boston, 88
    partners, 78
    on private currency, 68

Parker, Hayward, 22

Parker, John (Lord Boringdon), 102–103

Parker, Julia Ann Brown, 21, 22, 86

Parker, Pierpont, 20

Parker, Theodore, 22

Parker, Thomas, 103

Parker House. See Omni Parker House

Parker House Roll, 5, 10, 21, 29, 33
    Dutchess Divider, 31
    recipe, 26

Parker's Bar, 14

Parker's Restaurant, 18, 24, 76

Parkman, Francis, 47

Parris, Alexander, 78–79

Patrick, Deval, 10, 62

Patti, Adelina, 64

"Paul Revere's Ride" (Longfellow), 47

Pemberton Square, 82

Perry, John, 88

Person + Killian Photography, 40–41

Phan Van Khai, 33

Phillips, Wendell, 67

Pierce, Edgar, 35

Pine tree, state symbol, 103

Political clientele, 54–63

Powell, Colin, 10

Powers, Dave, 96

Prang, Louis, 68

Presidential Cookbook, The (Nesbitt), 29

Press Room (Omni Parker House), 40, 50, 54, 76

Punchard, Edward O., 78, 86

Quincy Market, 71, 79

Rascal King, The (Beatty), 58–59

Ray, Rachael, 10

Red Sox baseball team, 99

Revere House, 17, 78

Ribas, Joseph, 31, 76

Rice, Alexander Hamilton, 59

Richman, Hal, 8

Ricketson, Daniel, 46

Ritchie, Dave, 5

Robinson, Mary, 97

Rogers, Isaiah, 78

Rogers, Will, 29

Romney, Mitt, 62

Rooftop Ballroom (Omni Parker House), 40, 68, 76

Room and board, origin of term, 27

Roosevelt, Eleanor, 26, 28

Roosevelt, Franklin Delano, 10, 26, 28, 60

Rowling, Robert B., 87

Rudolph, Paul, 83

Ruth, Babe, 10

Sacco, Paul, 8, 63

Sanzian (chef), 18, 24–25, 31

Saturday Club, 10, 16, 44, 45, 46, 47, 50, 51, 53

Savage, Minot J., 22

Scarlet Letter, The (Hawthorne), 42, 44

Schiffer, Claudia, 72

Schlesinger Library on the History of Women in America, 28

School Street, 13–15

Scollay Square, 7

Scrod, origin of term, 26

Seasholes, Nancy S., 90

Sewall, Henry F. Collection, 88

Shagbark Farm, 90–91

Shawmut House, 17

Shelton, Frank, 8

Sherrard, Andrew, 8, 71, 92–93

Sherrard, Glenwood, 8, 71, 86, 92–93

Sherrard, Jessie Lumsden, 71, 92

Shire, Lydia, 31

Simonson, Eric, 59

Smoking rooms, 46

Somerset Hotel, 92

Song of the Lark, The (Cather), 53

Stewart, Martha, 33

Stuart, Dave, 76

Stuart, F. T., 48

Suffolk County Courthouse, 82

Sumner, Charles, 88

Tab (newspaper), 50

Temple (Maine), 20

Terry, Ellen, 64

Theatrical activities, 64–69

Thoreau, Henry David, 10, 46

Ticknor, William D., 45

Torres, Antonio, 8

Tower, Lori, 5

Tracy, Spencer, 58

Tremont House, 19, 78

Tremont Temple, 64, 68

Tremont Theatre, 42, 48, 64

TRT Holdings, Inc., 87

Truong Quang Duoc, 33

Tsongas, Paul, 62

Tufts University, 5, 79

Twain, Mark, 5, 51

University of Massachusetts, Dartmouth Campus, 83

Valley View Farm, 34–39, 91

Victoria Hotel, 78

Walden (Thoreau), 26

Ward, Artemus, 27, 67

Warren, George Kendall, 51

Washburn, William, 78, 79

Washington, George, 15

Wason Memorial Building, 35

Webster, Daniel, 44

Weddings, 40–41

Wendell, Jacob, 16

West, Adam, 10

Wharton, Edith, 52

Whipple, Joseph Reed, 34–35, 86, 90, 92

Whipple, Rose Gay Higgins, 35, 90

Whiskey Magazine, 59

White, Jasper, 31

White, Kevin, 6, 71

White House, 28

White House Diary (Nesbitt), 28

Whittier, John Greenleaf, 47

Wickford, Ralph T., 83

Williams, Ted, 10

Winiker, Annette, 73, 75, 76

Winiker, Bill, 74, 76, 77

Winiker, Bo, 74, 76, 77

Winiker, Ed, 73–77

Winiker Band, 73–77

X, Malcolm, 7, 10, 31

Yastrzemski, Carl, 10

Young's Hotel, 34, 78, 90

Omni Parker House

60 School Street

Boston, Massachusetts 02108

tel: 617/227-8600

fax: 617/742-5729

www.omnihotels.com

For reservations please call 1-800-THE-OMNI

Printing: Jeffrey Warren, Emerald Graphics; Indexing by Eileen Quam, M.L.S., Finedex Indexing Services